Sambeawesome's Coloring Book: Sea Creatures

Copyright © 2017 by Samantha Segal

All rights reserved. No part of this publication may be reproduced, distributed, or transmitted in any form or by any means, including photocopying, recording, or other electronic or mechanical methods, without the prior written permission of the author, except in the case of brief quotations embodied in critical reviews and certain other noncommercial uses permitted by copyright law.

Additional exceptions include personal use of colored artworks made from the line work provided in this book. Non-edited or direct copies of the line work may not be shared in any manner as listed above.

Attribution is appreciated if any colored creations are shared. Credit cannot be claimed for the line work and must be given to the author.

For information contact:
sambeawesome@gmail.com
https://twitter.com/sambeawesome

Book and Cover design by Samantha Segal

ISBN-10: 1975896645
ISBN-13: 978-1975896645

First Edition: September 2017

Table of Contents

Introduction..5

Let's Get Coloring:..6
   Oarfish...7
   Portuguese Man O' War...9
   Cuttlefish..11
   Lionfish..13
   Imaginary...15
   Knobby Seahorse..17
   Leaf Scaled Sea Snake...19
   Sea Pen...21
   Imaginary...23
   Octopus...25
   Fangtooth Moray...27
   Feather Star..29
   Striped Dolphin...31
   Euryleptidae..33
   Angler Fish..35
   Sea Spider..37
   Manta Ray...39
   Atlantic Sea Raven..41
   Spotted Seal..43
   Pacific Lamprey..45
   Imaginary...47

Tutorials:..49
   Transparency..50
   Transfer...52
   Coloring Basics...54
   Digital Coloring..58
   Copic Coloring..66

About the Artist..72

Introduction

Hello there! Phew, now that we've broken the ice, welcome to my first ever coloring book! The theme is mermaids because...why not? (I mean, everyone likes mermaids, right? Right?)

I've always thought the idea of making a coloring book would be a fun one, and I'm so happy to have finally had the chance to do it! It certainly wasn't as easy as I expected, but that made it no less rewarding! :)

I'm also really happy to help represent the LGBT community, especially my fellow polys. You guys are an inspiring group of people and I'm glad to be a part of it. Let's spread the love!

Whether or not you consider yourself an artist, I hope you can gather some enjoyment and relaxation from this book. Pick out your tools of choice, maybe some soft music, candles, and just chill for a few hours while you let your imagination loose.

If you'd like to share any of your creations on social media, be sure to use the hashtag: #sambemermaid so we can all find them! I'd love to see what ya'll create!

Have fun!

Let's Get Coloring!

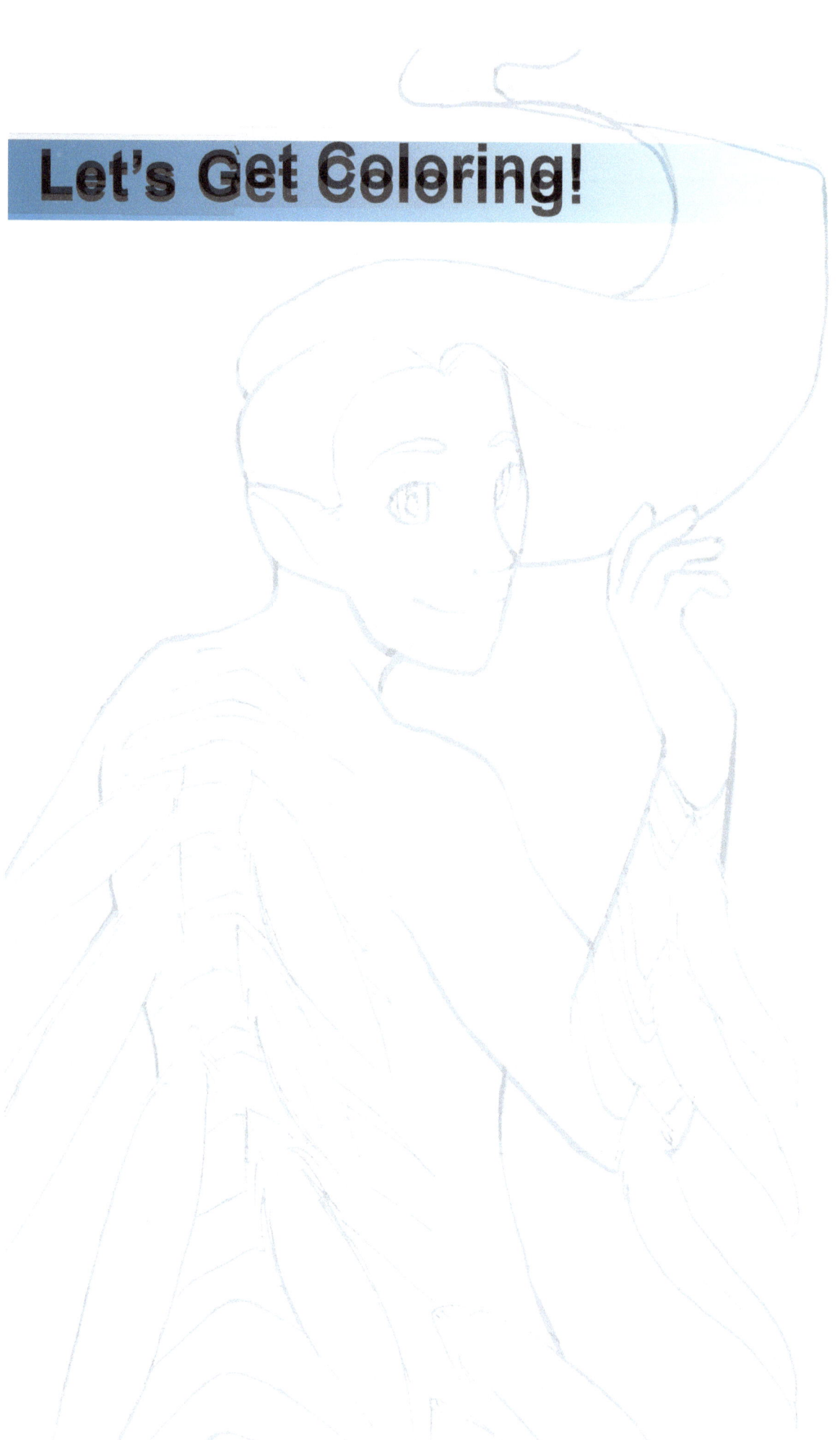

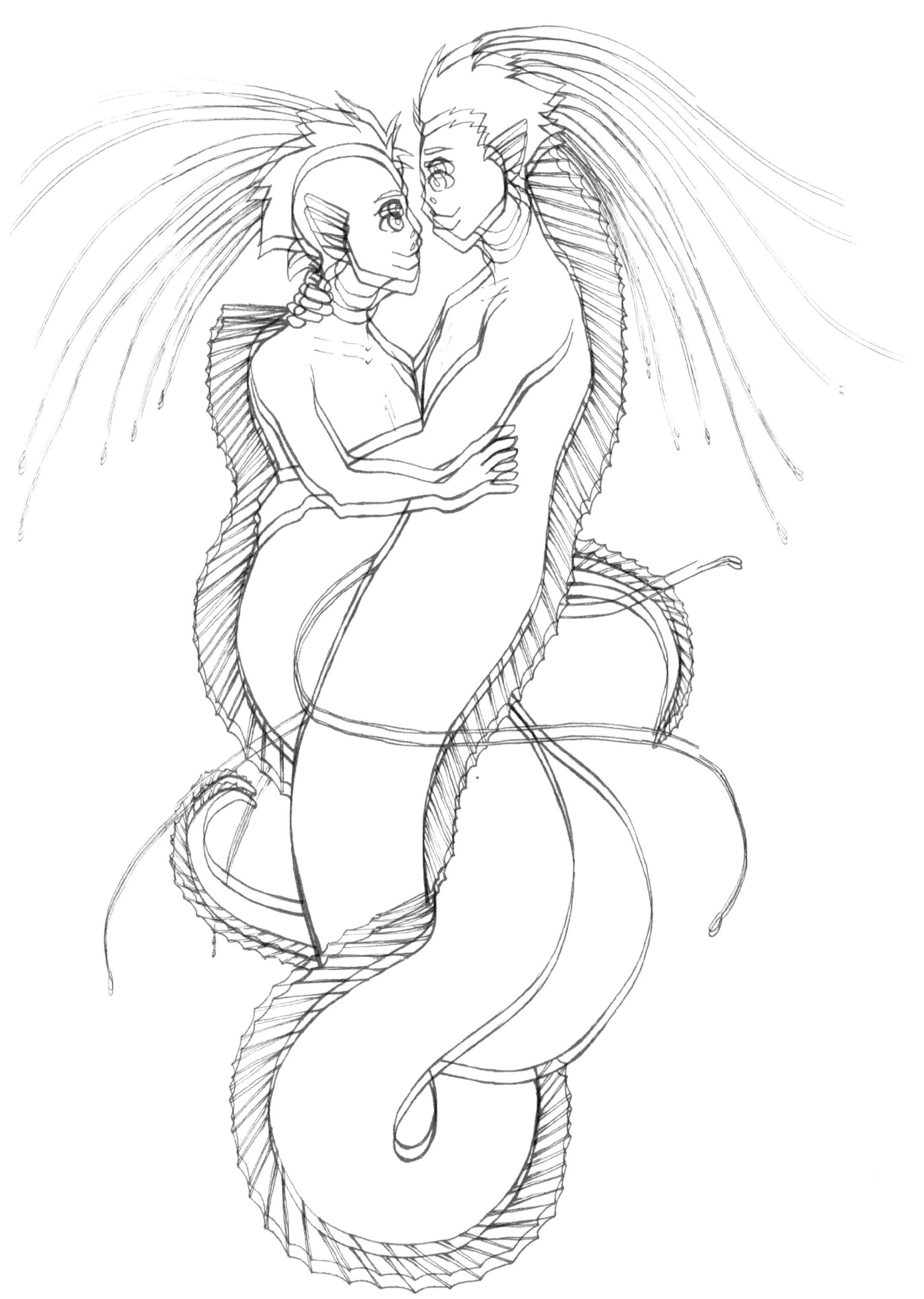

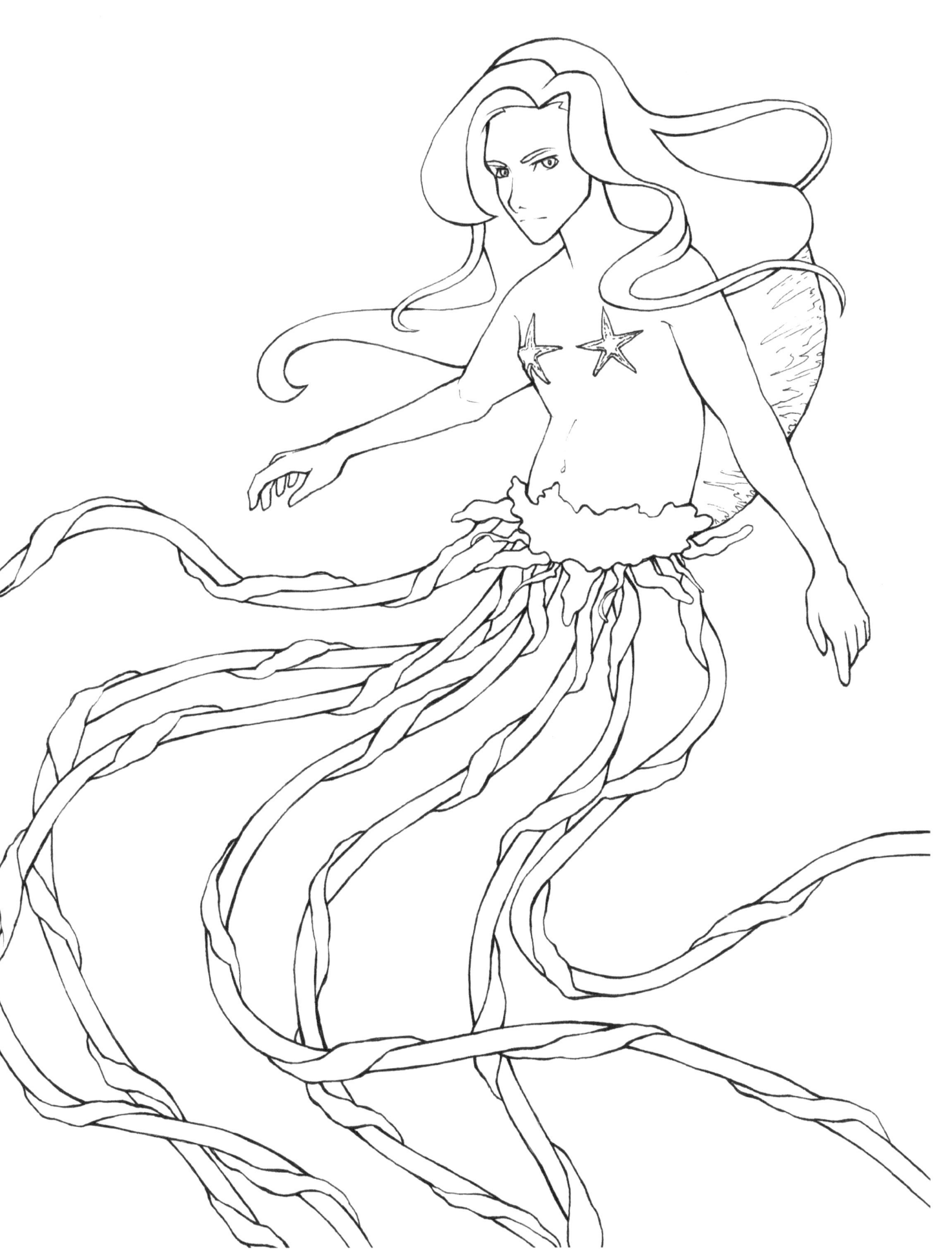

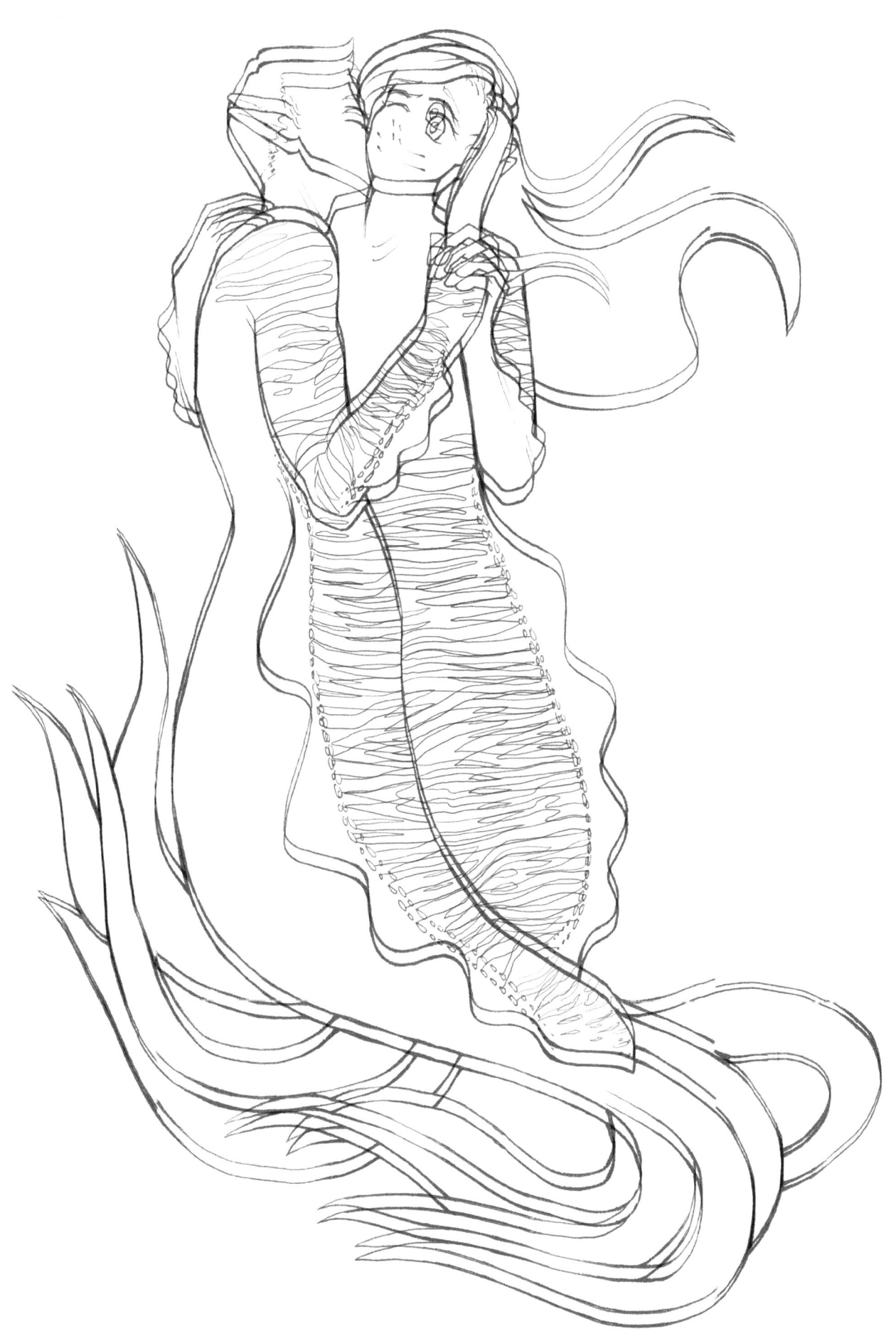

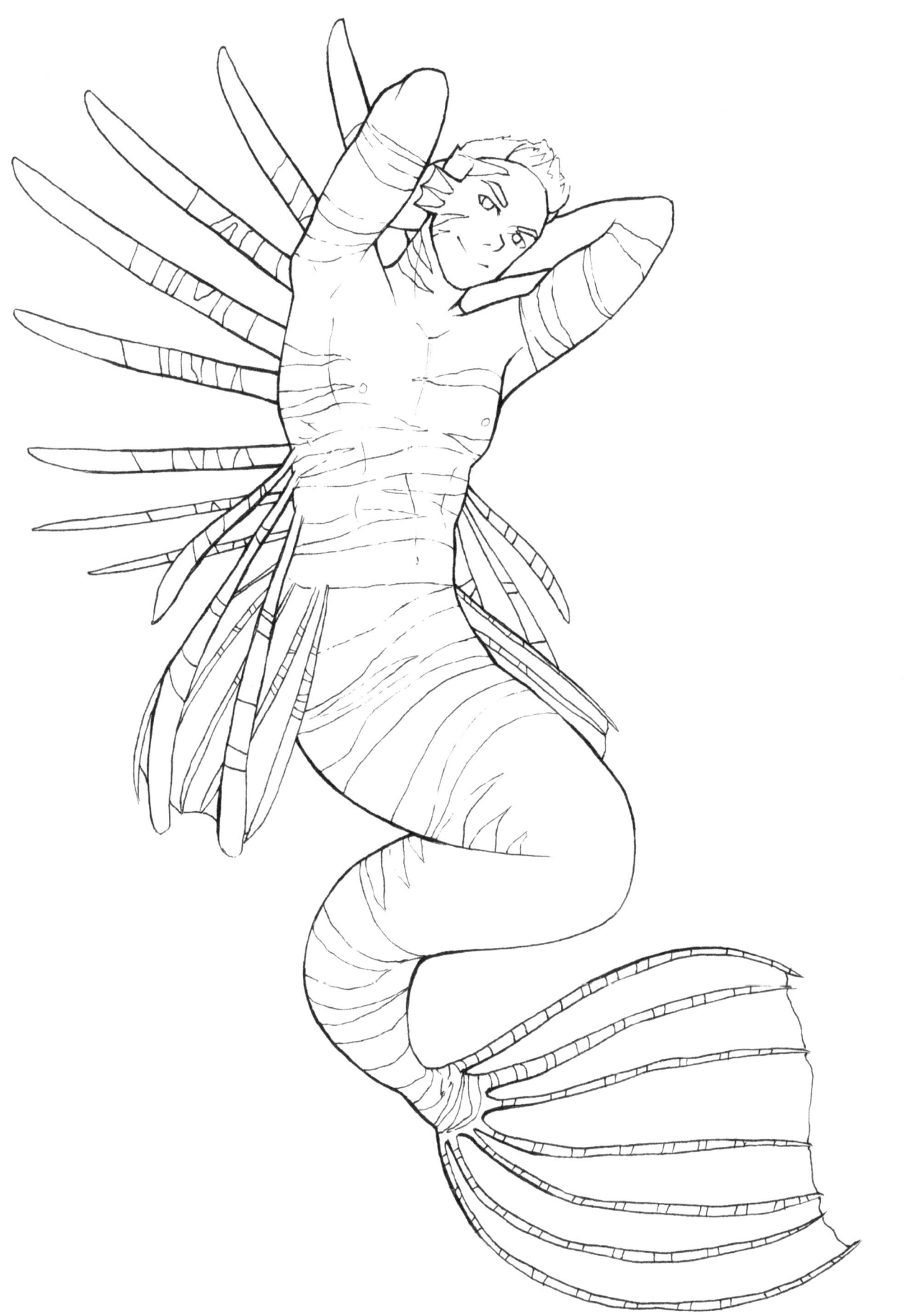

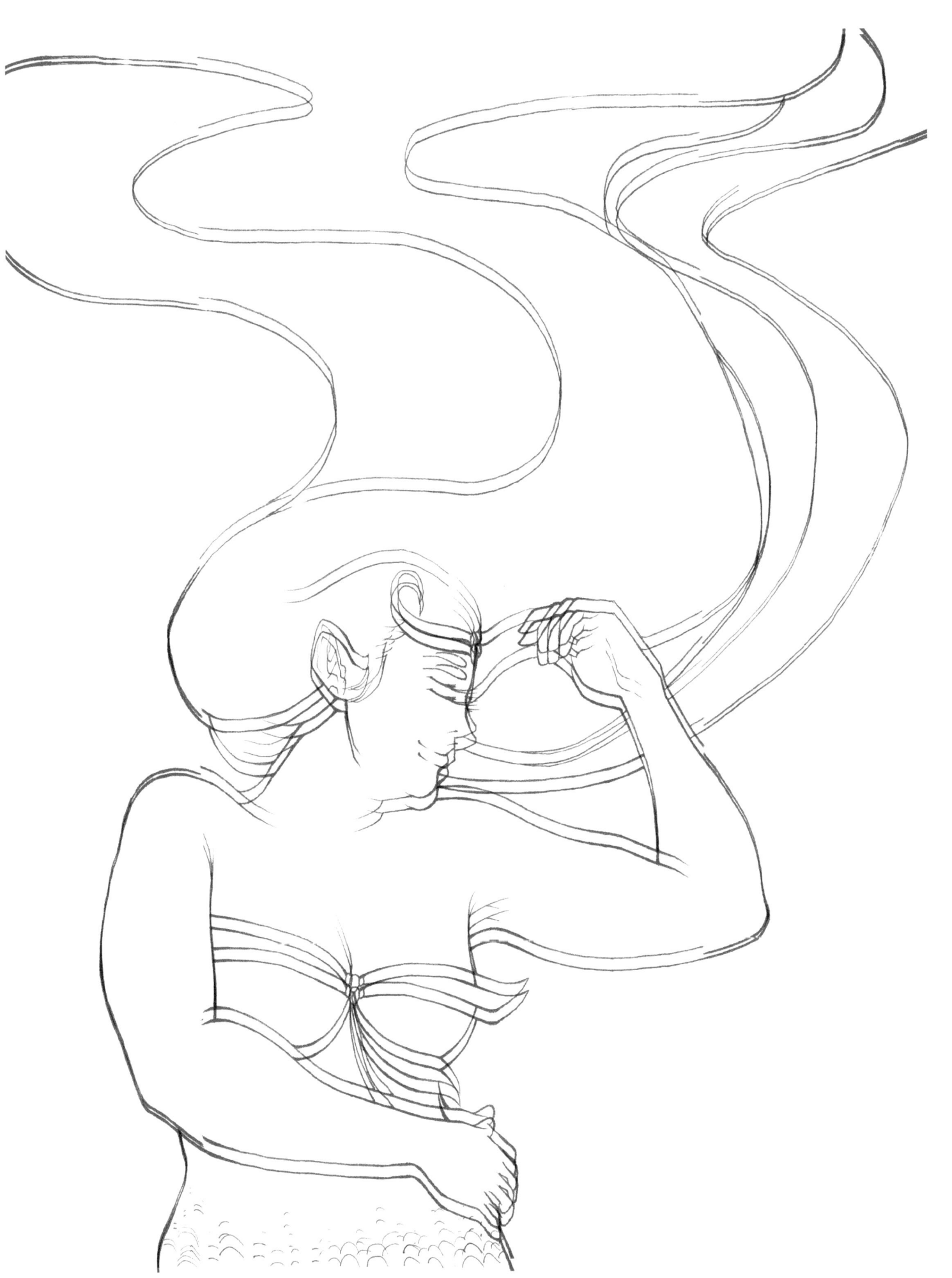

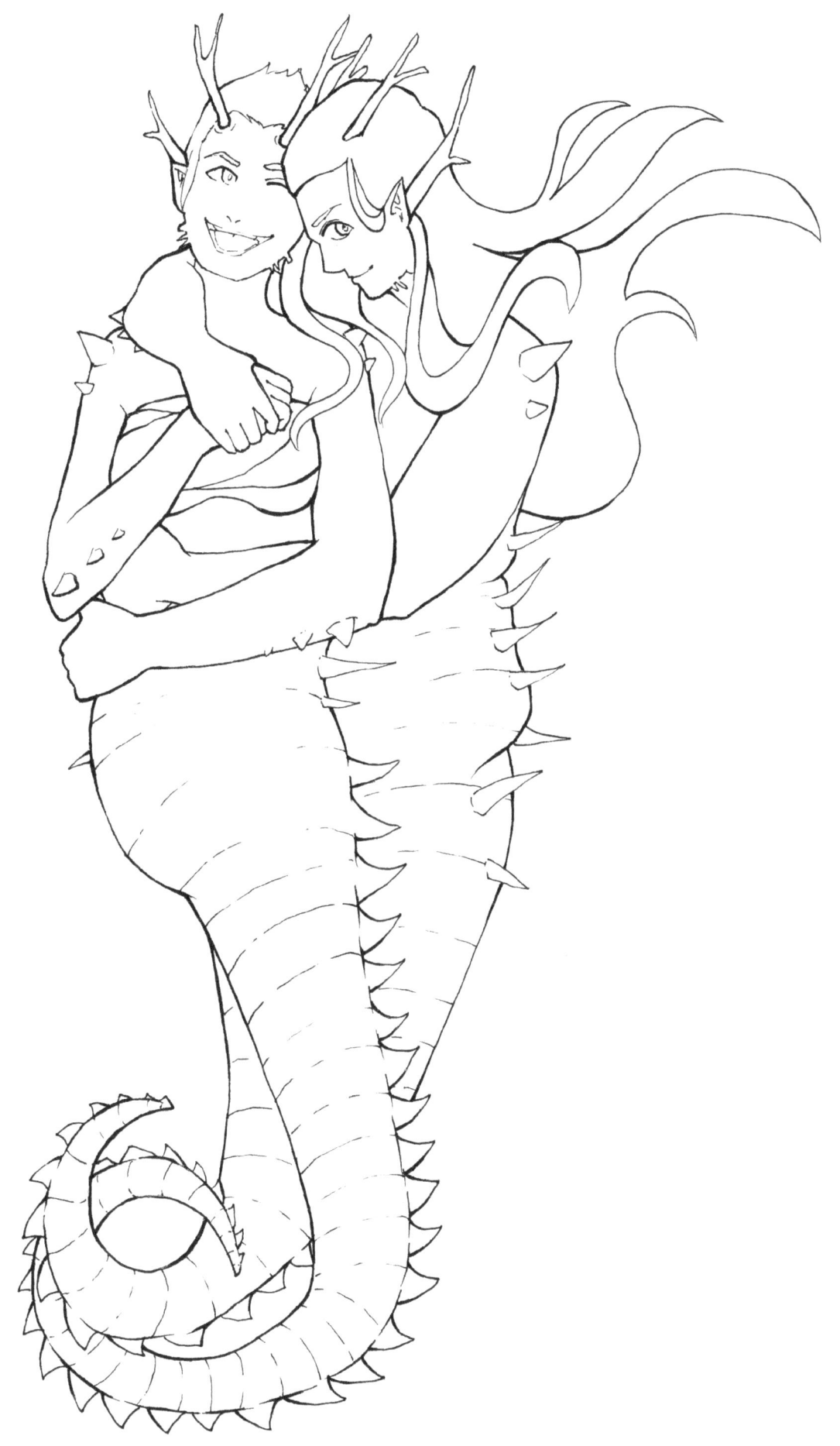

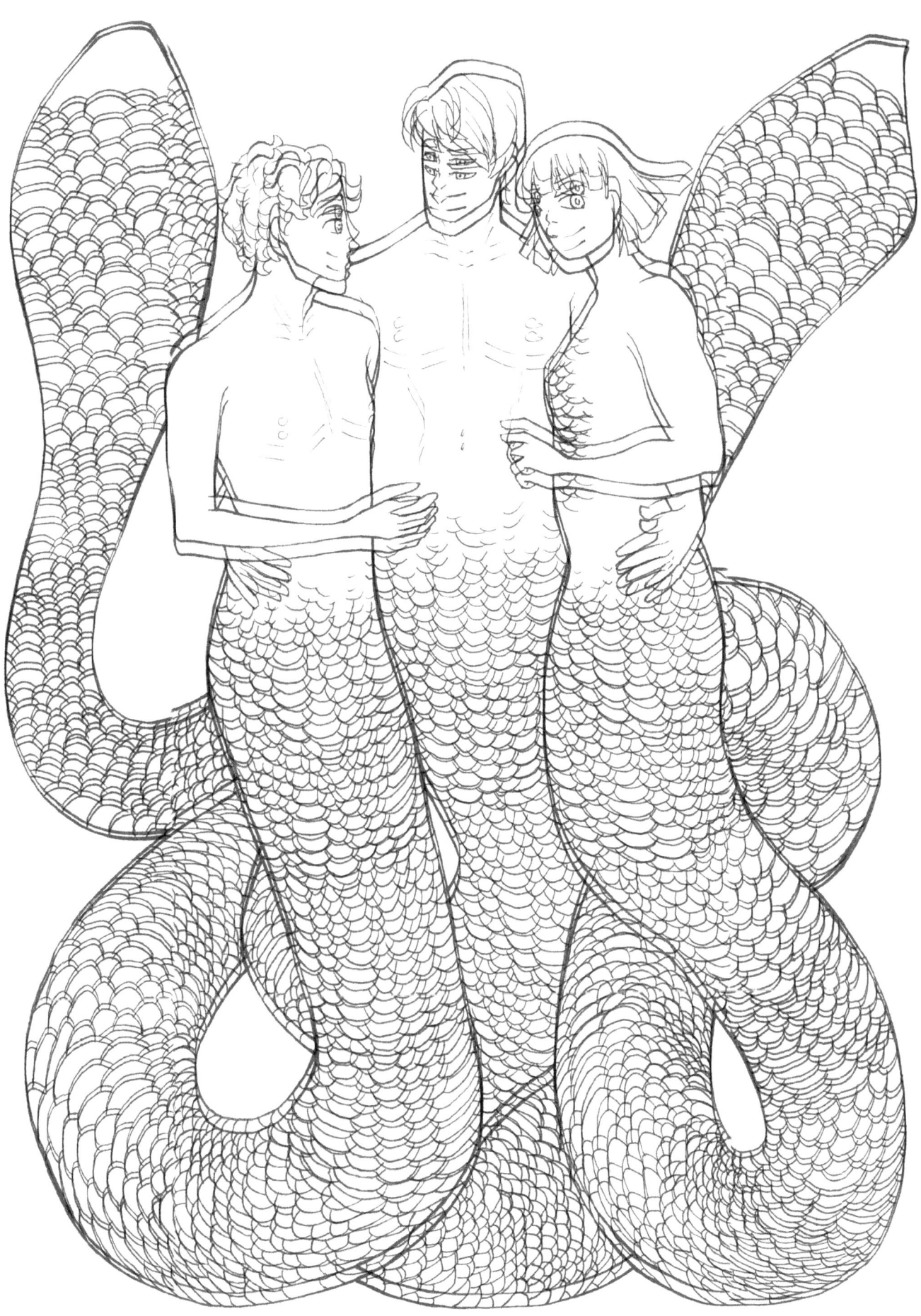

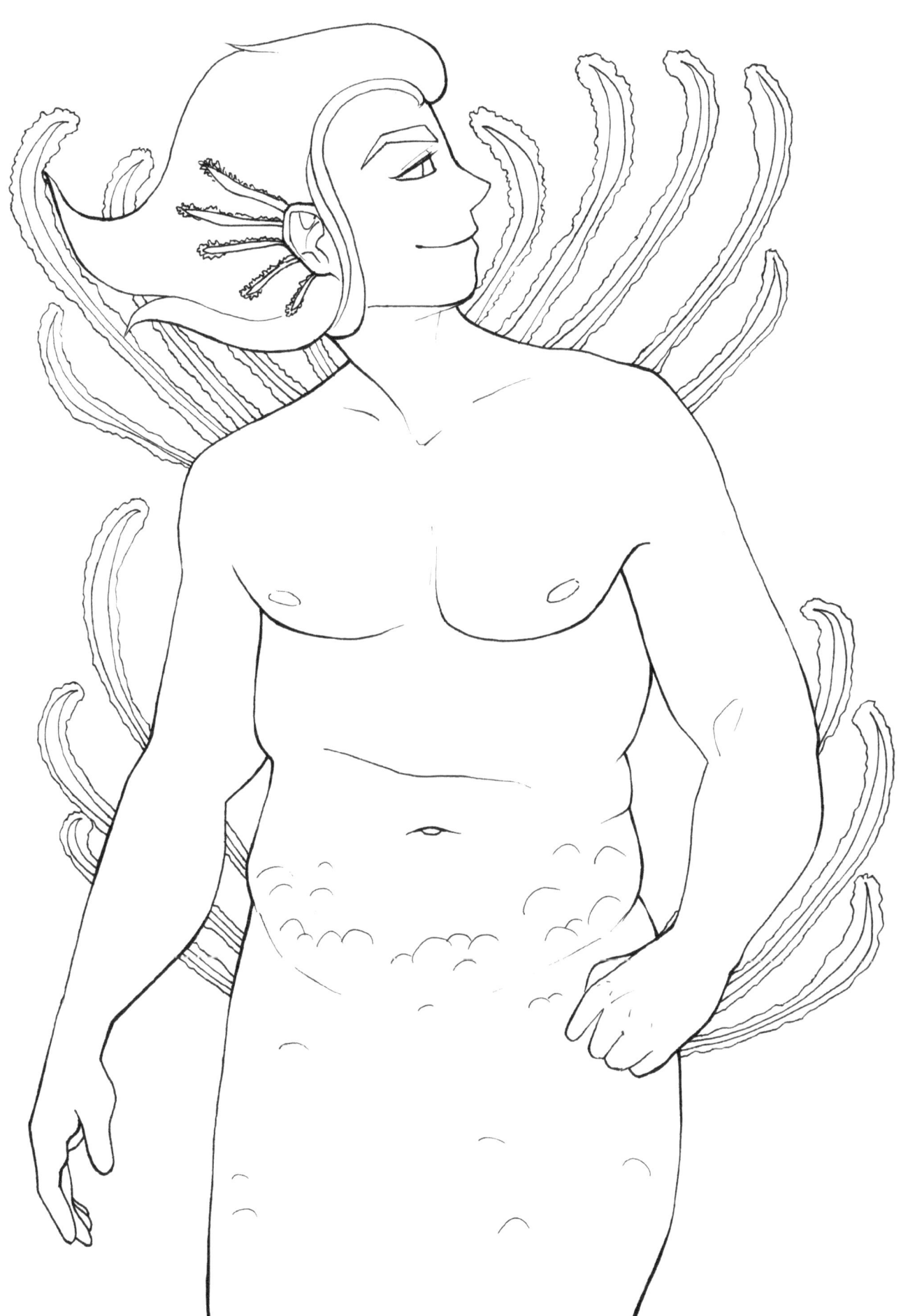

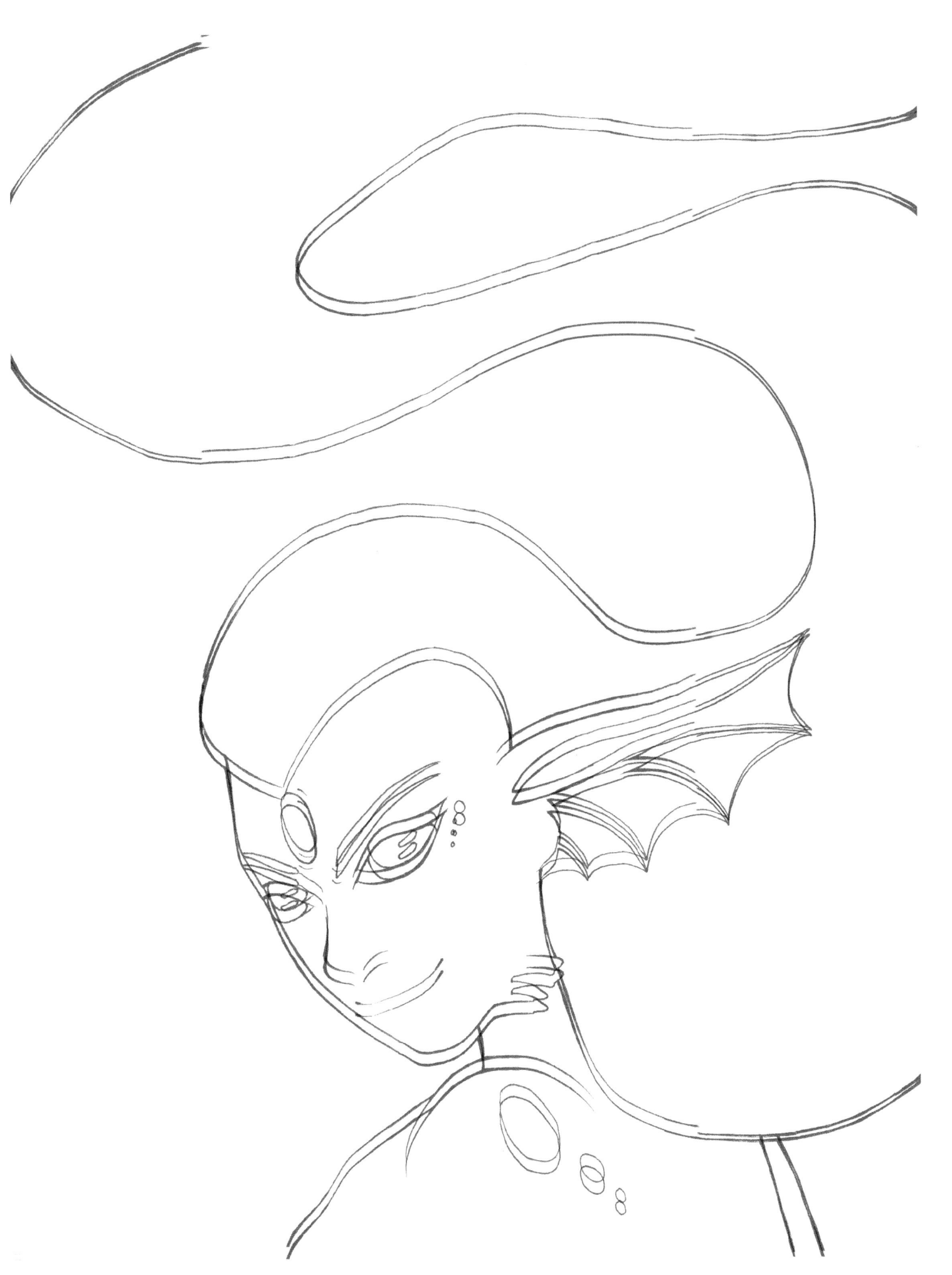

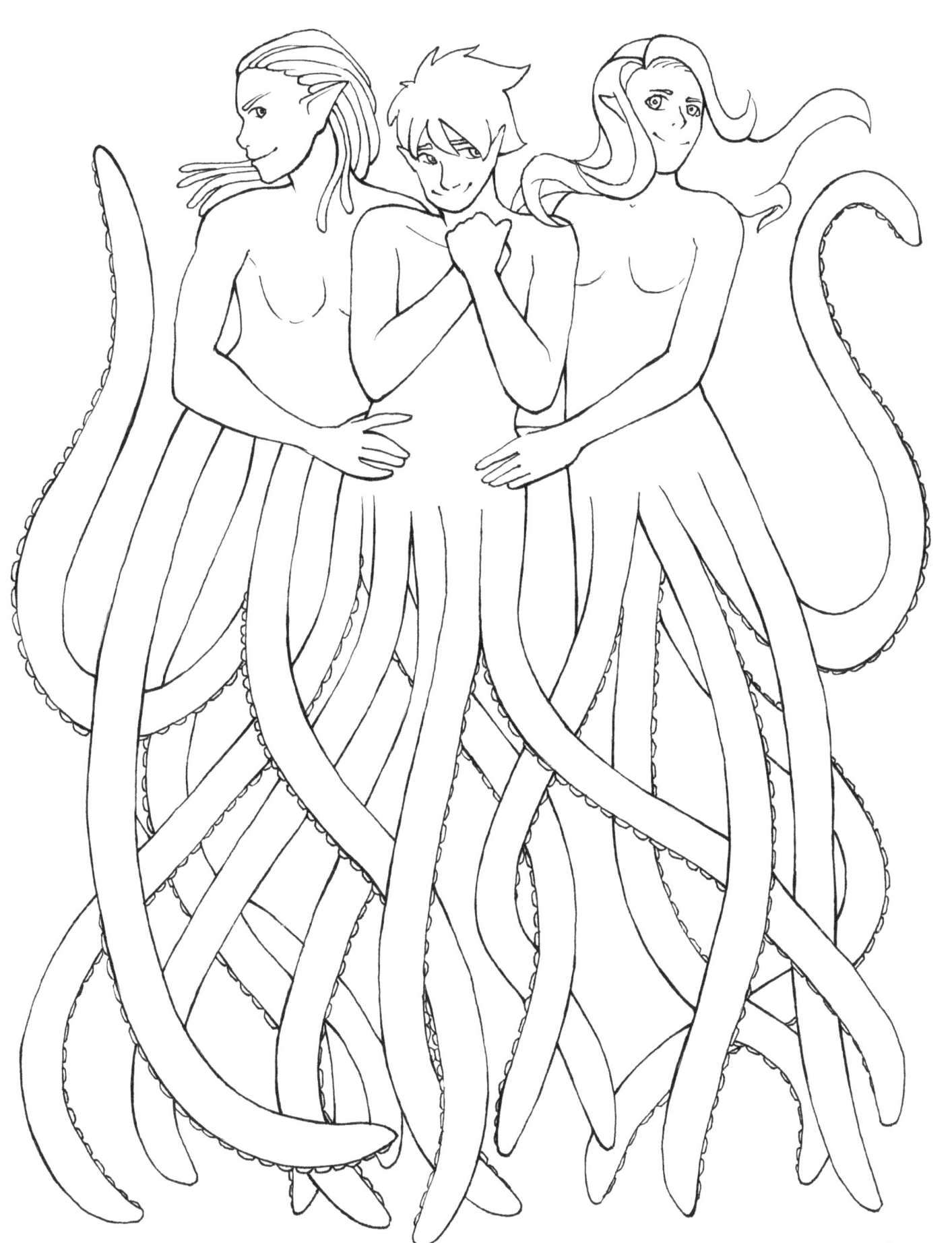

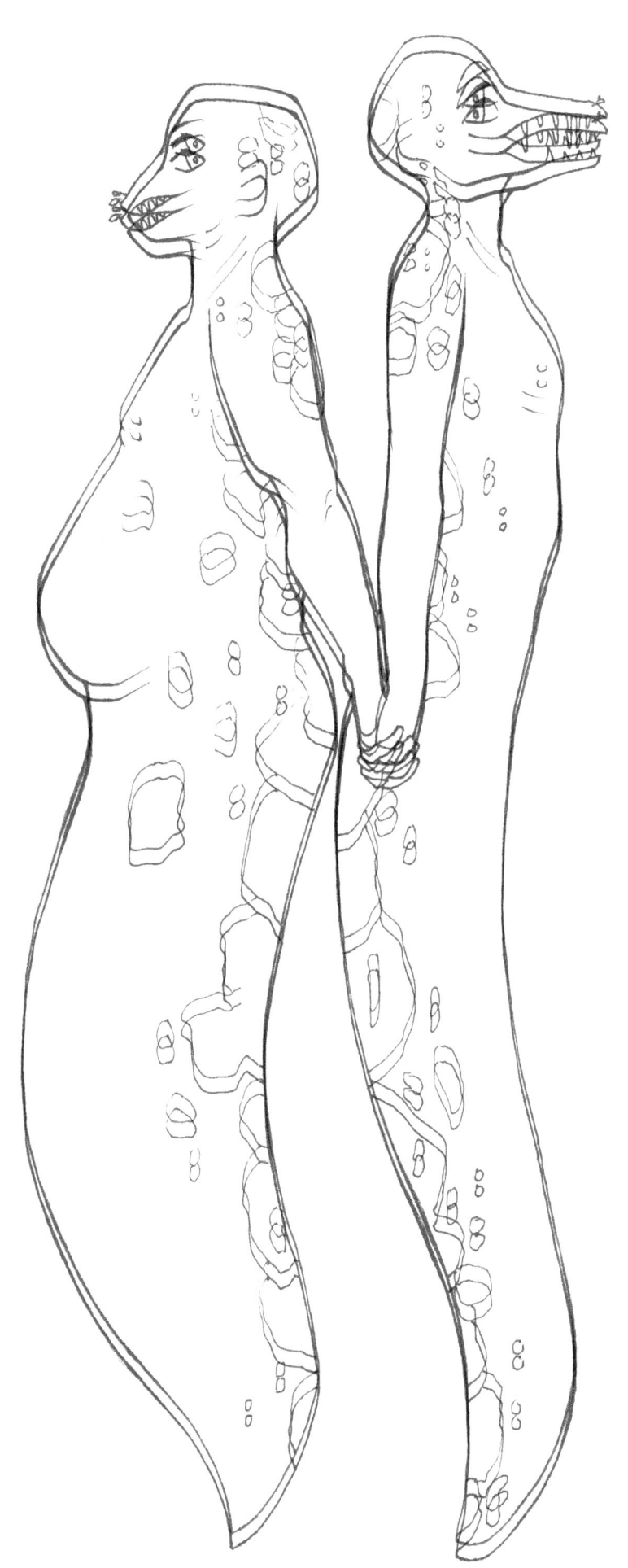

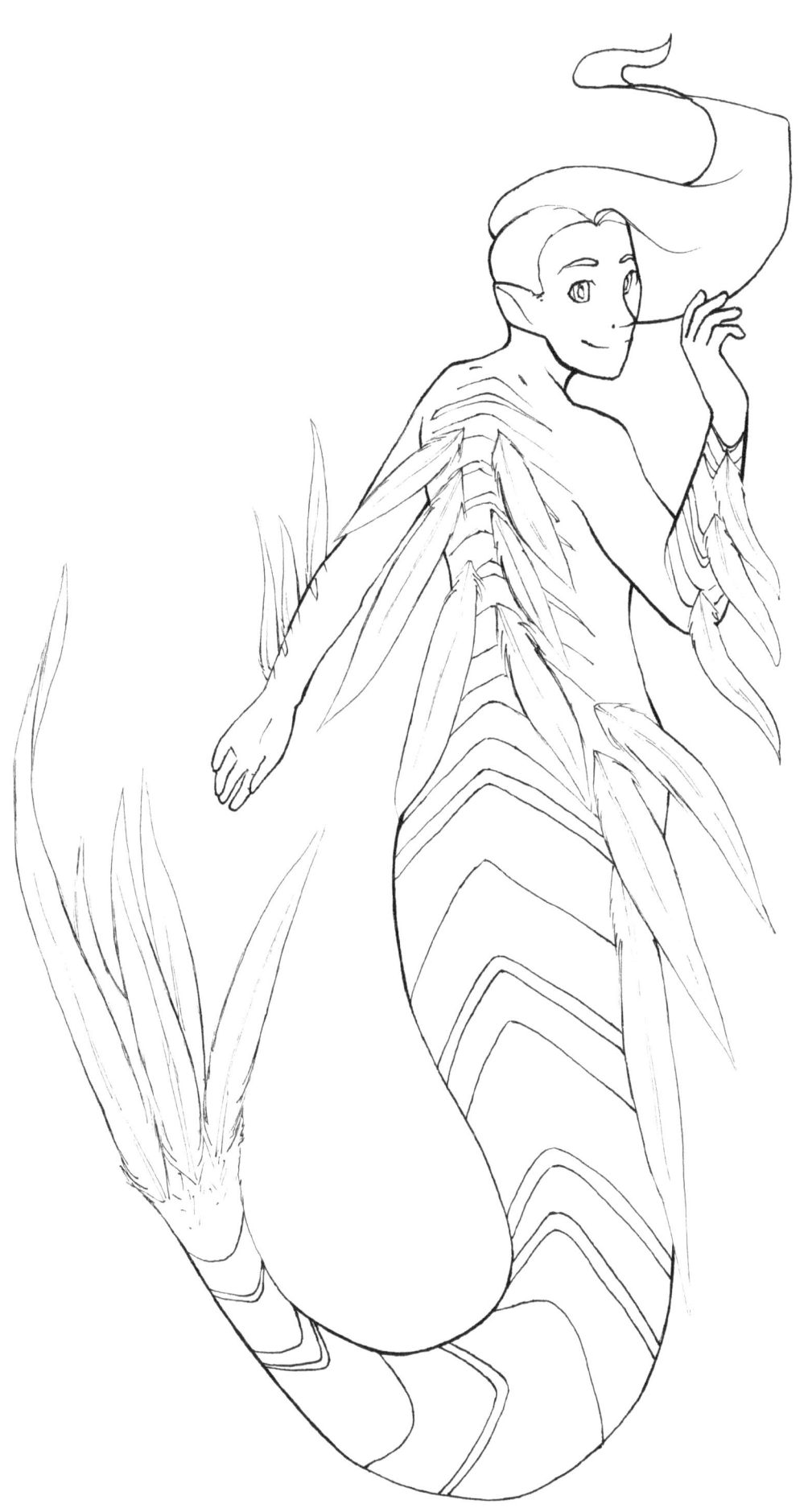

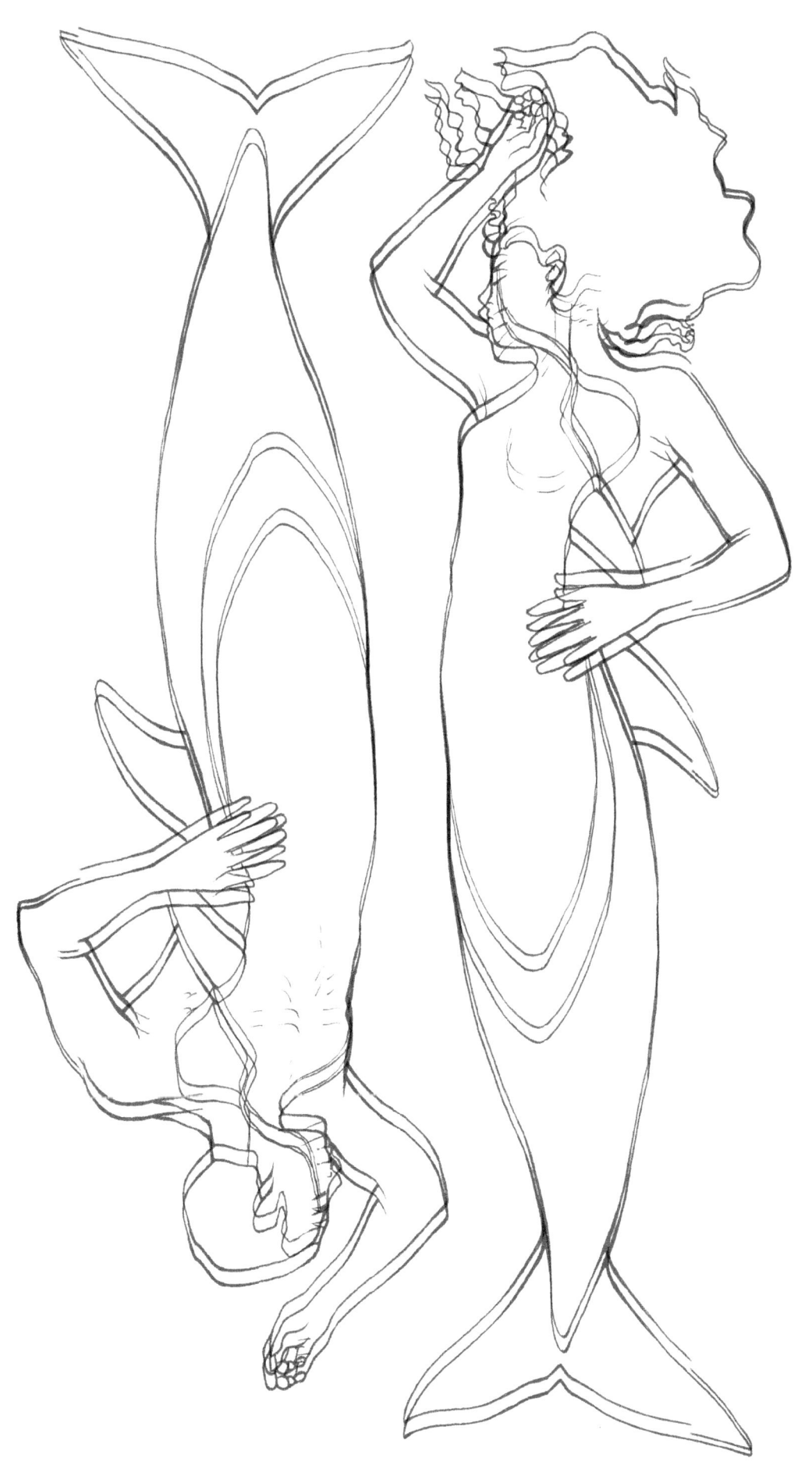

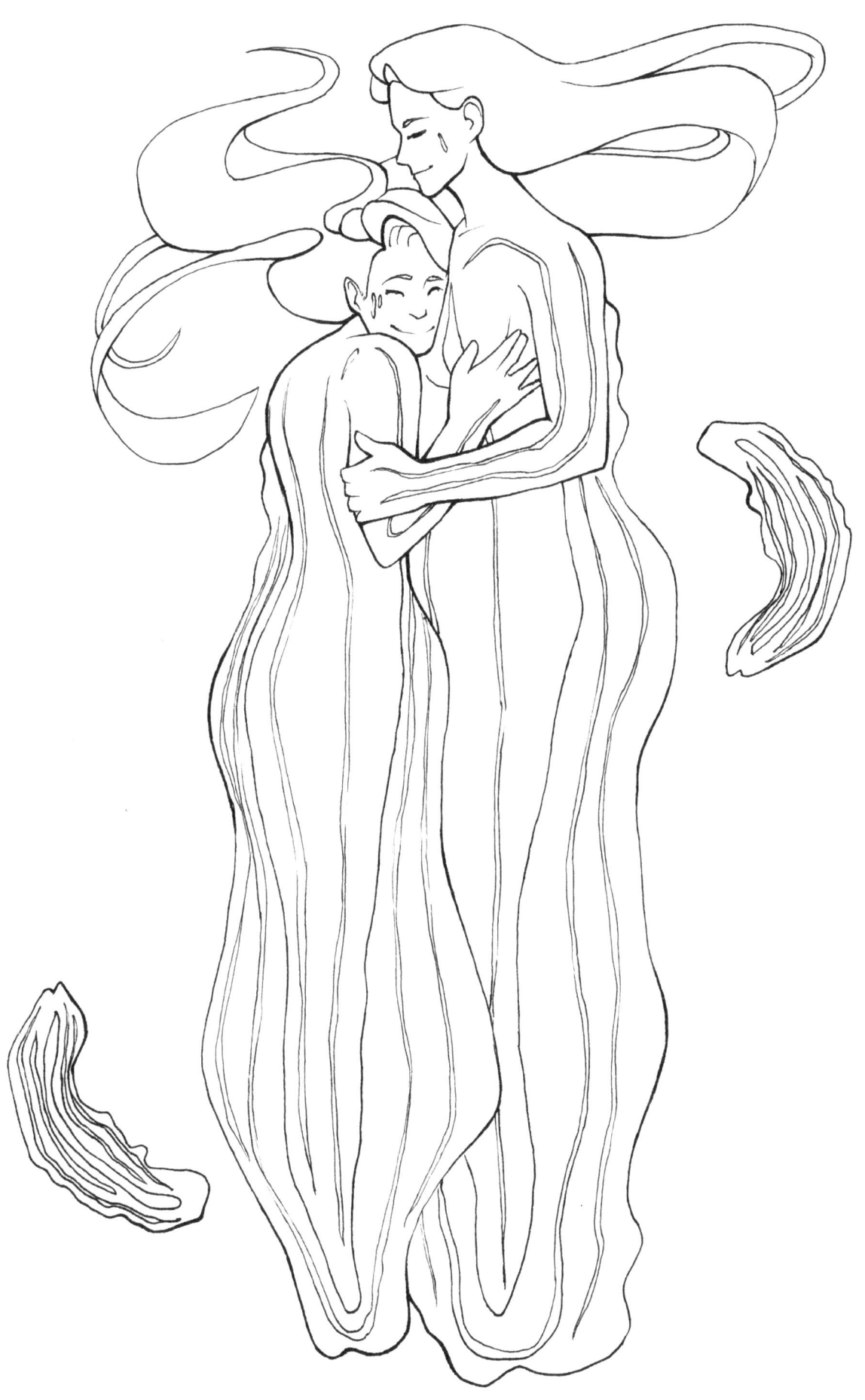

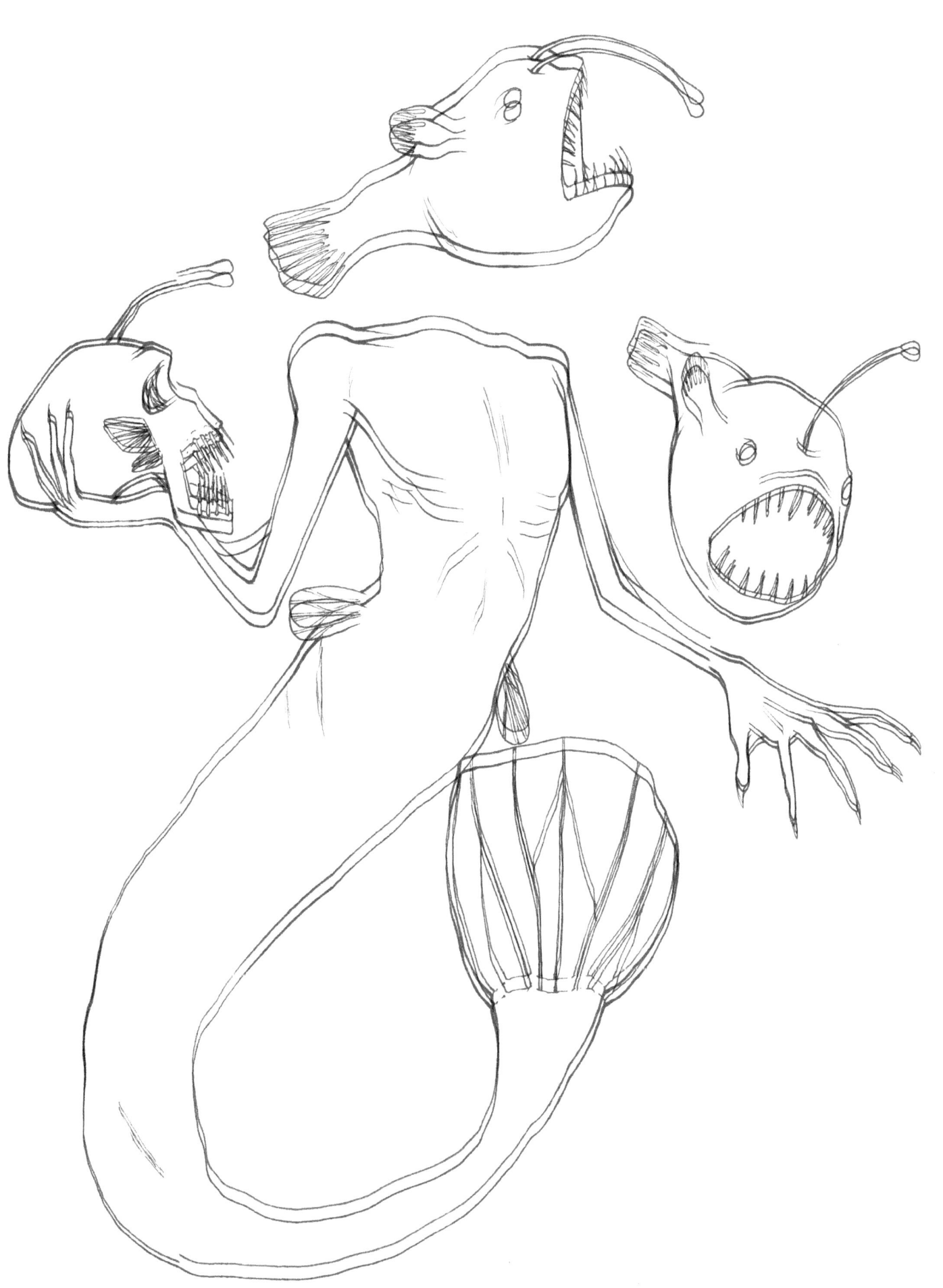

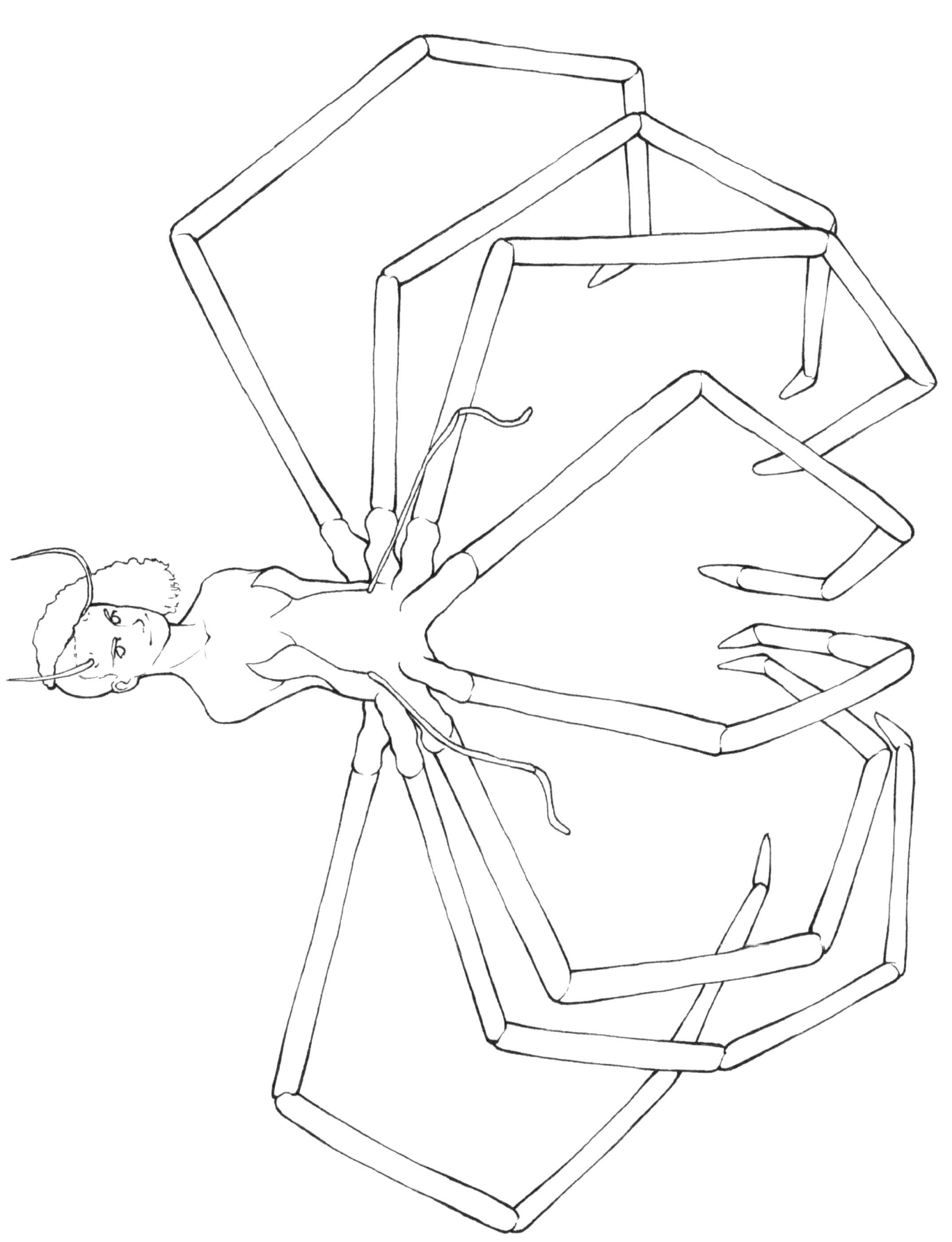

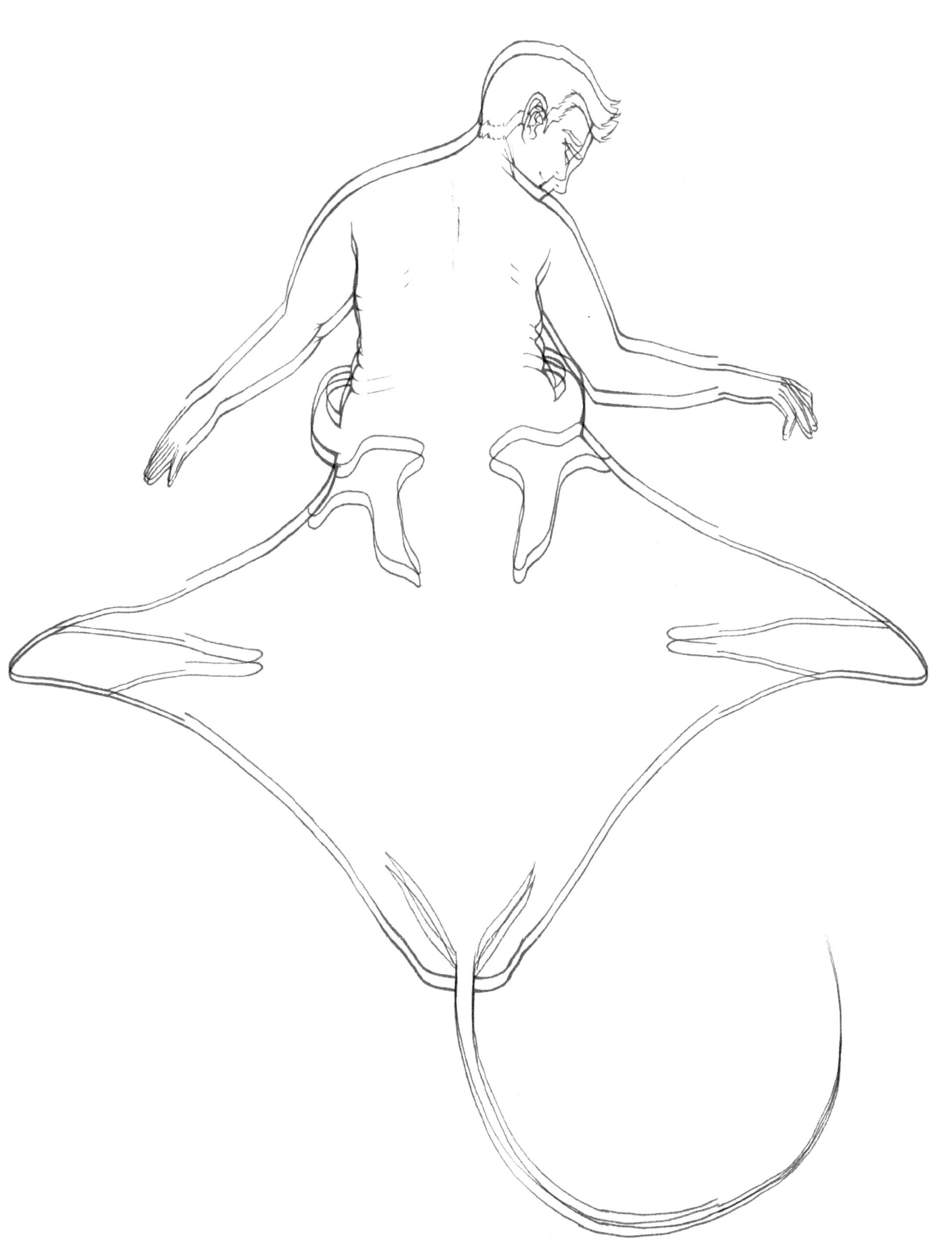

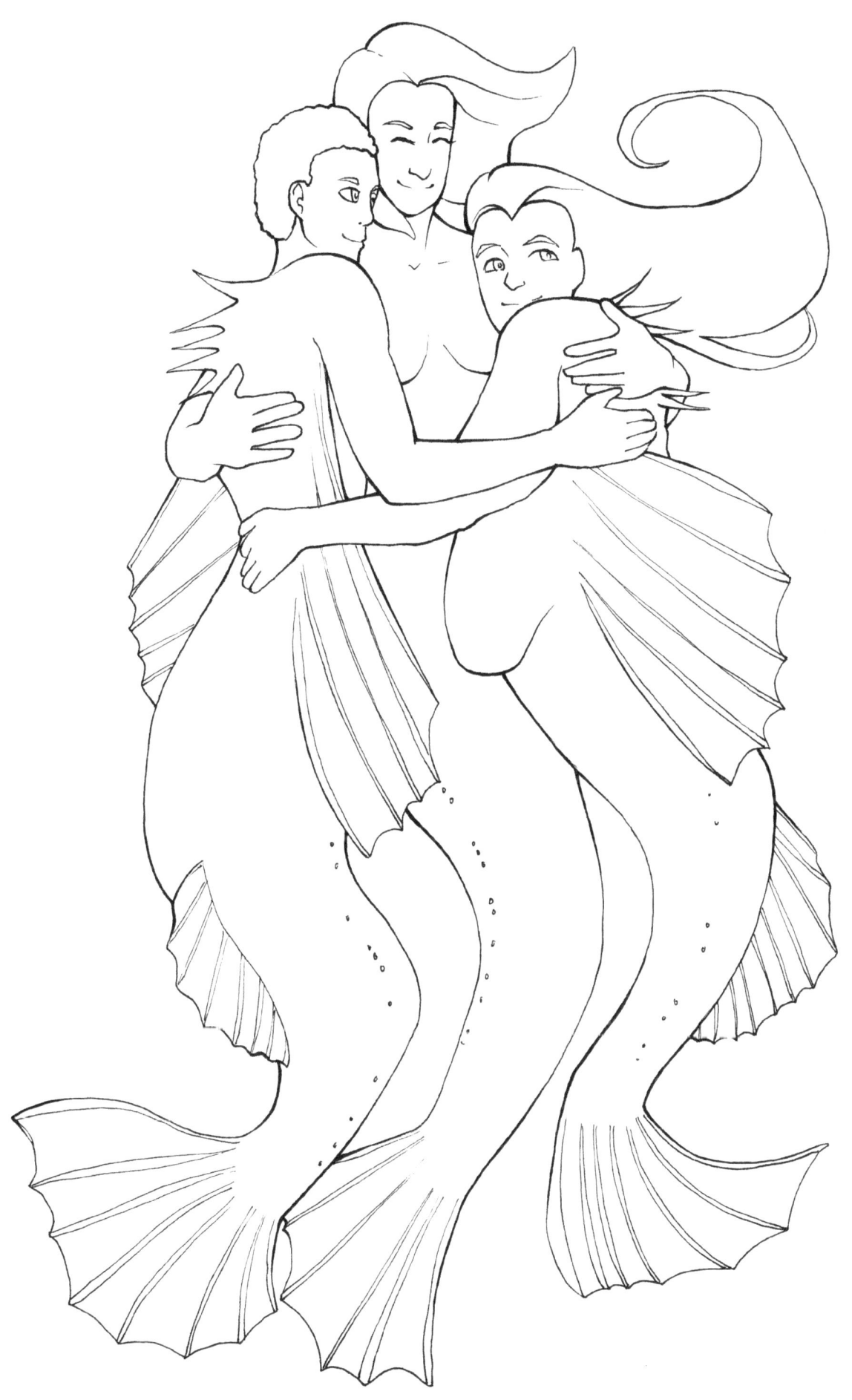

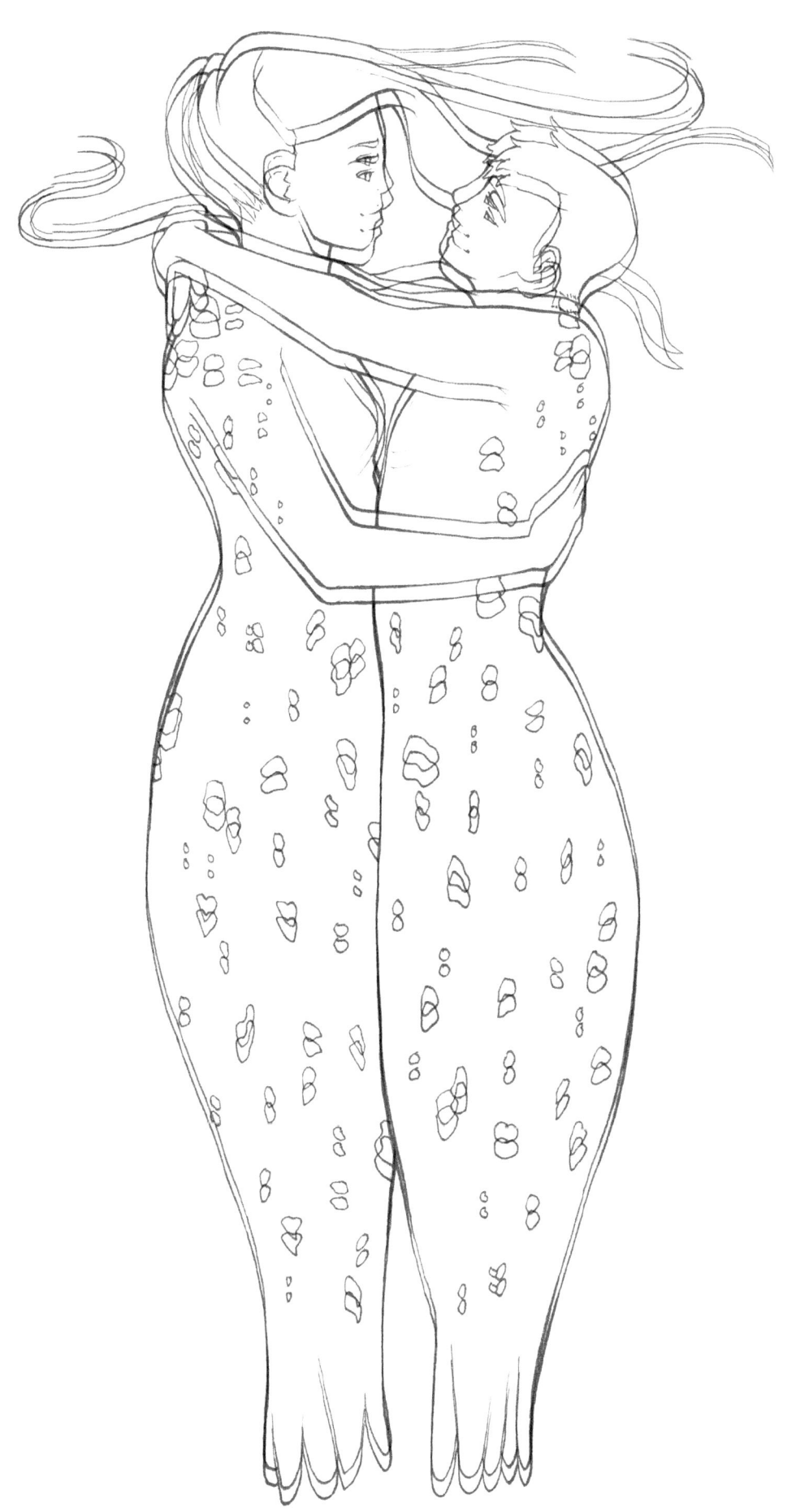

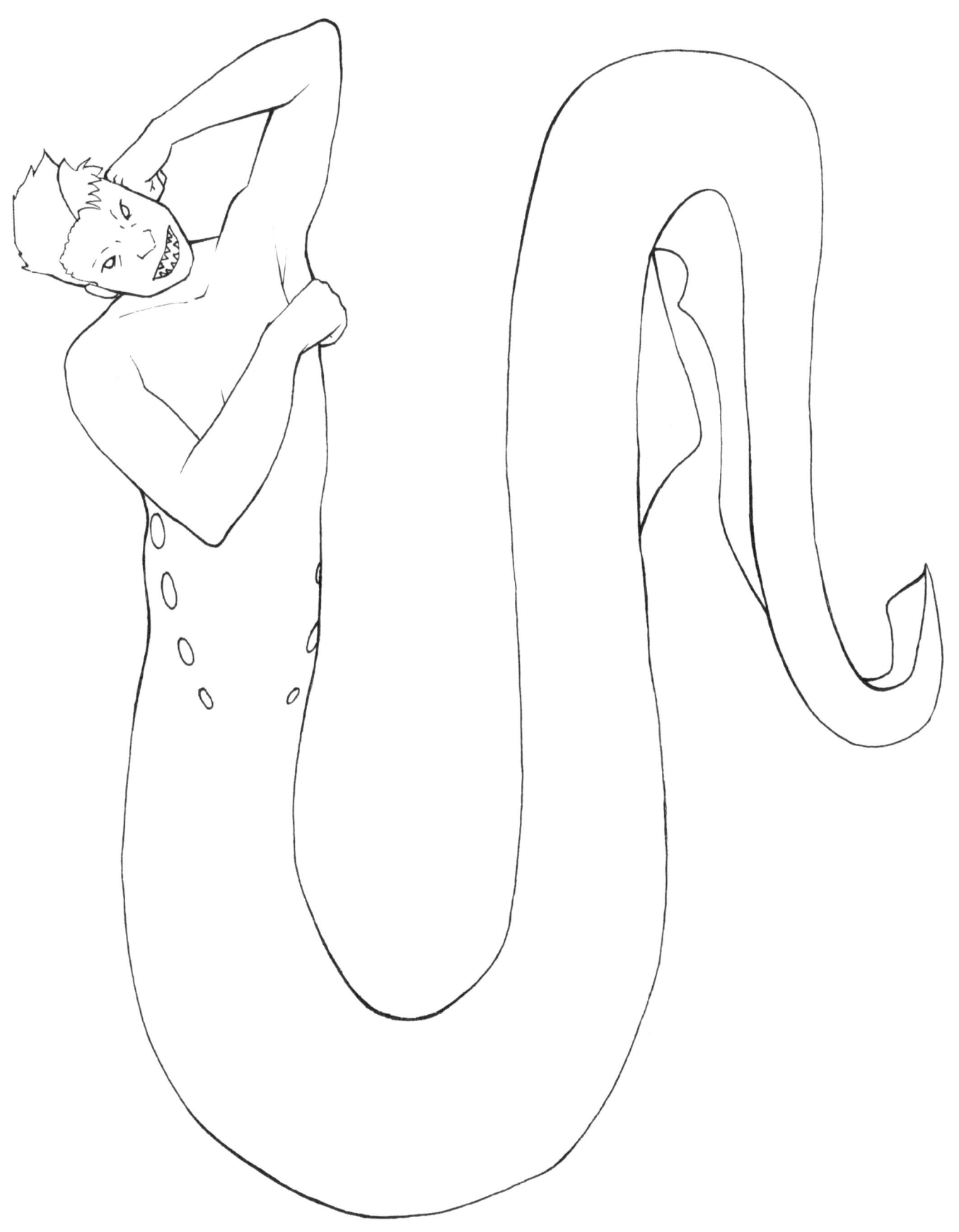

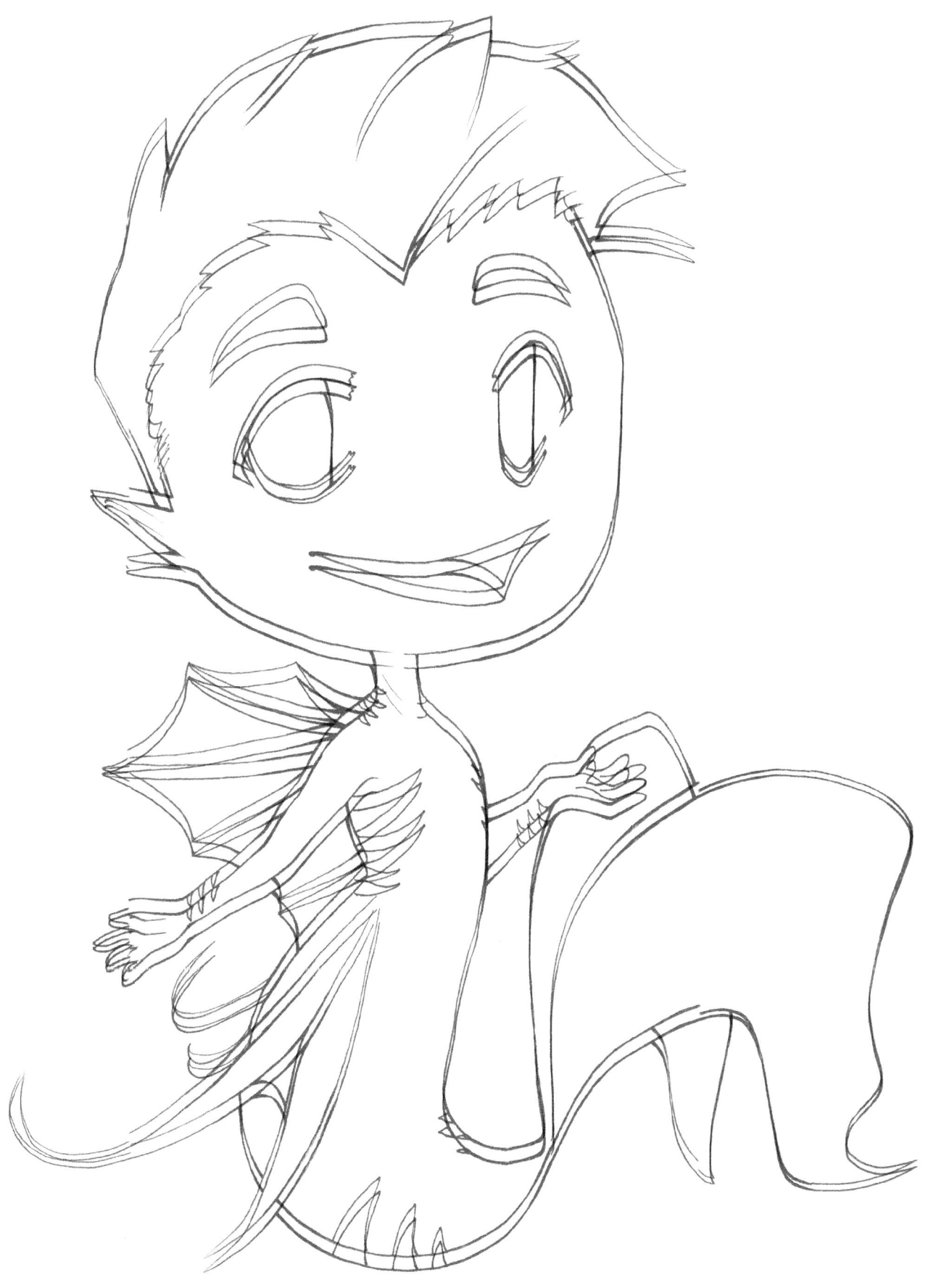

Tutorials!

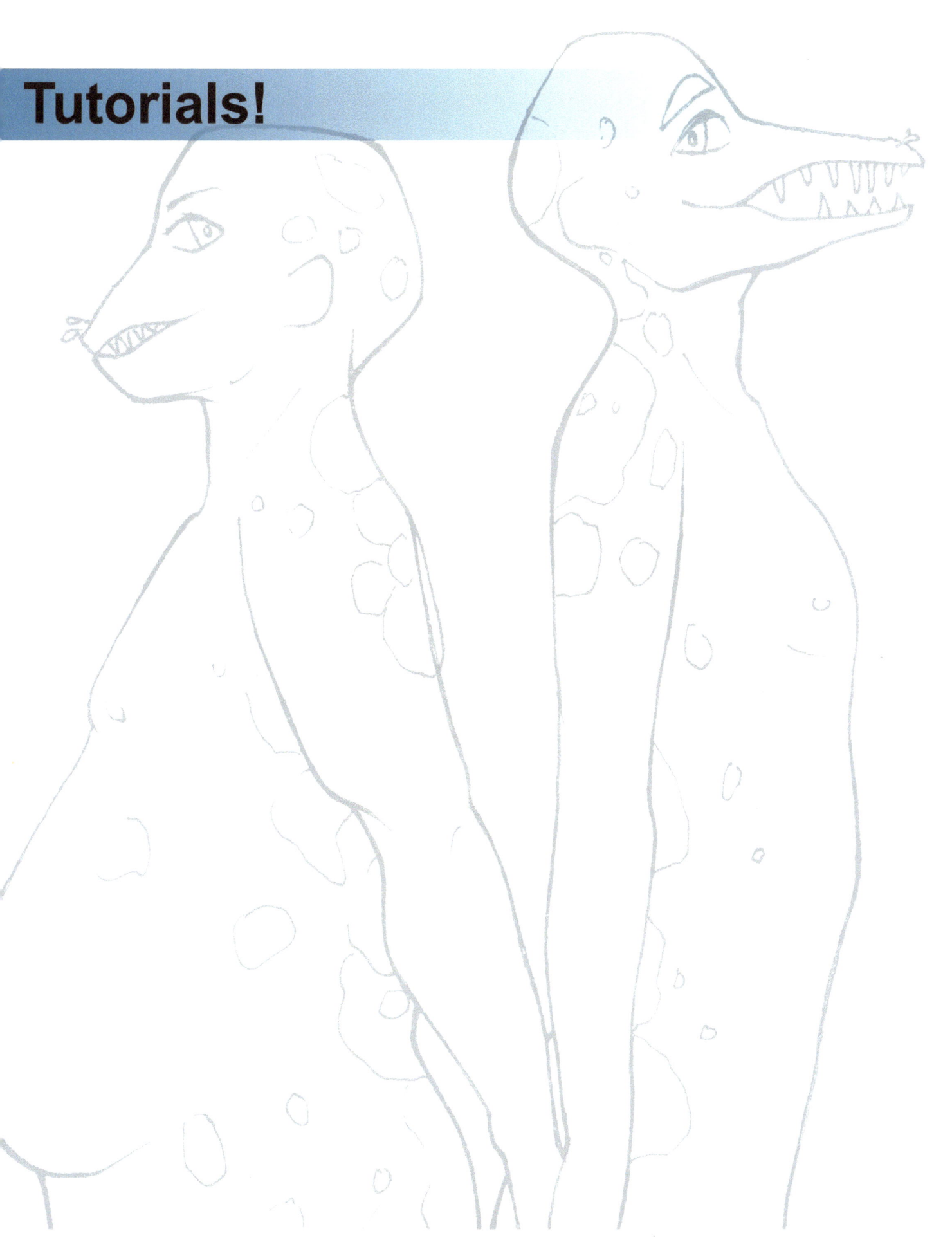

Transparency Tutorial:

Like I'm sure many digital artists have encountered in their lifetime: white backgrounds can be pain! I'll show you here how to rid yourself of that nuisance. I'll be using Adobe Photoshop.

Note: There are multiple ways to remove a white background, this one is just my favorite :D)

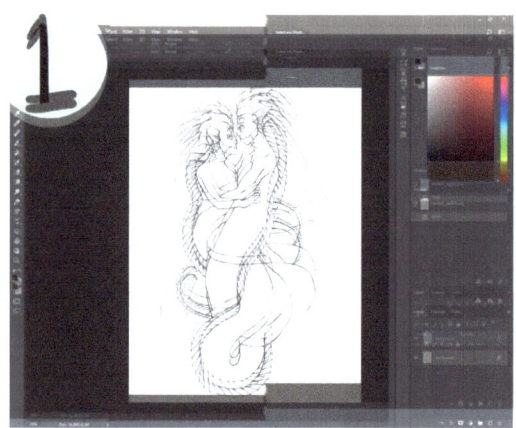

Go ahead and open up the file.

Duplicate the layer:
-Drag the layer to the new layer icon.
-CTRL/CMD + J
-Layer -> Duplicate Layer

I do this to have a safe copy of the original file.

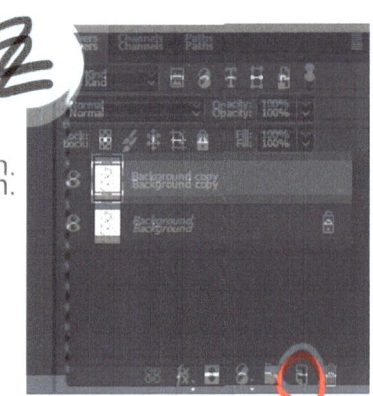

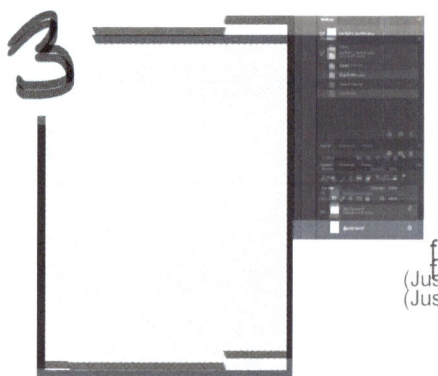

Cut the layer:
-CTRL/CMD + X
-Edit -> Cut

This saves a copy for you to paste later.
(Just be sure not to copy anything else in the mean time! xD)

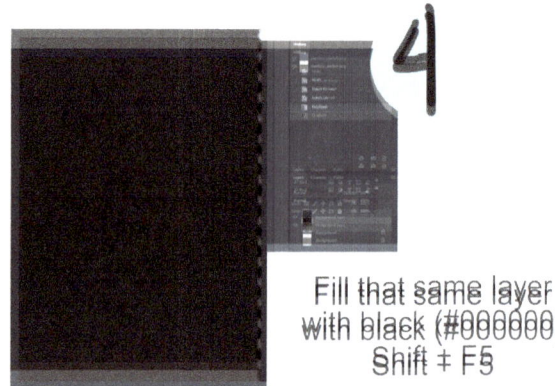

Fill that same layer with black (#000000)
Shift + F5

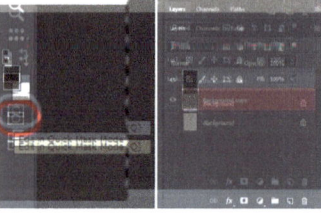

We're going to make a "Quick Mask" by hitting the "Q" key or by clicking the "Quick Mask Mode" button in the tool bar.

Paste the linework onto the same layer:
-CTRL/CMD + V
-Edit -> Paste

It should look like this:

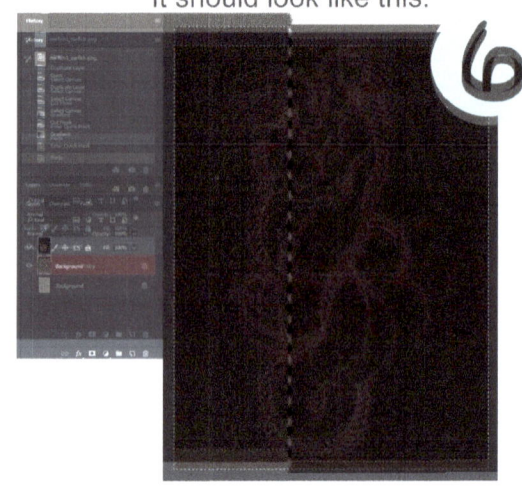

TIP:

Don't have Photoshop?

Manga Studio 5:
Edit -> Convert Brightness to Opacity

Paint Tool Sai:
Layer -> Luminance to Transparency

Transparency Tutorial: cont.

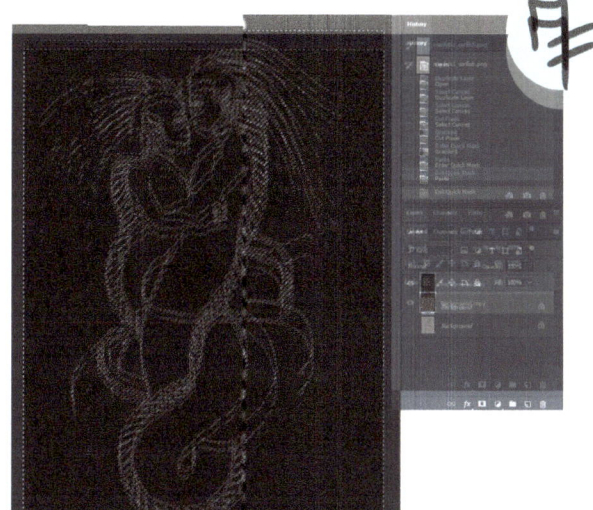

Exit the "Quick Mask" the same way you edited it. Hit "Q" or click on the "Exit Quick Mask" button on the bottom of the tool bar.

It should outline the artwork like this:

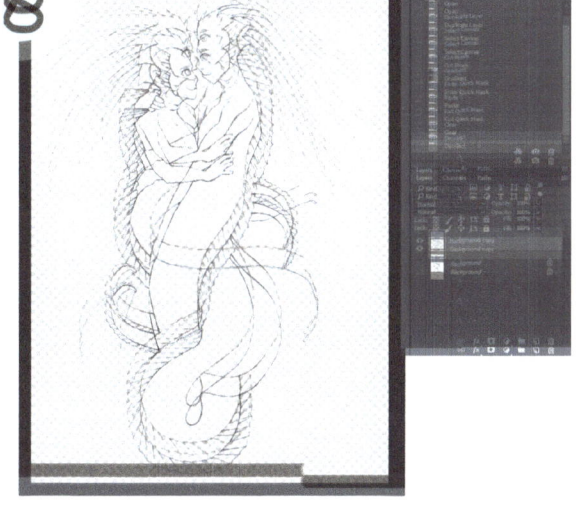

Clear the canvas:
- Hit the "Delete" key
- Edit => Clear
- CTRL/CMD + X

And you're DONE!

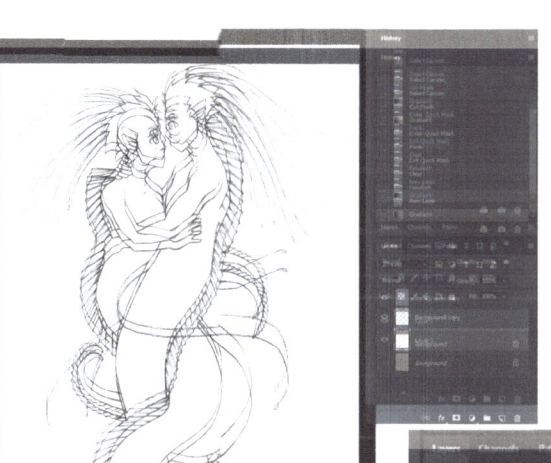

I added back in a white background behind the separated lineart layer so it's easier to see:

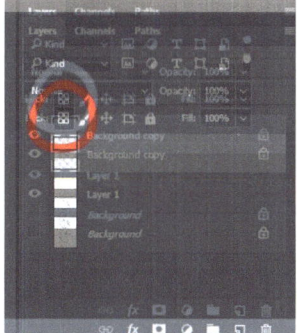

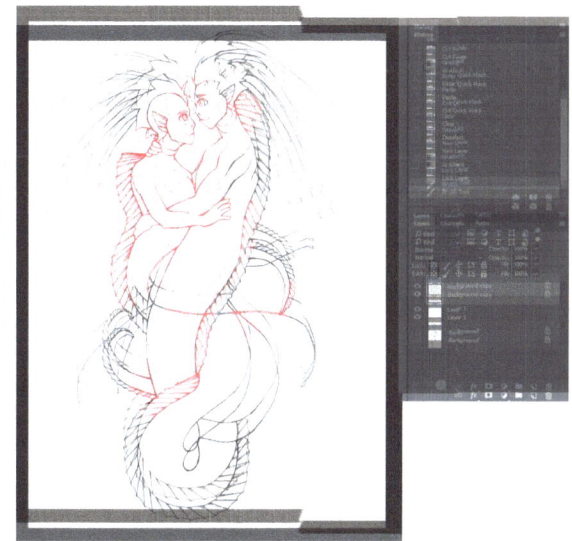

Locking the layer, you'll notice that anywhere you paint stays inside the lines!

Transfer Tutorial:

For those of you who are picky about what surface you work on, this tutorial is for you! I'll show you how to take these line works and put them on other papers or canvases!
(If you have the physical book book, I recommend scanning the page for ease of transfer.)

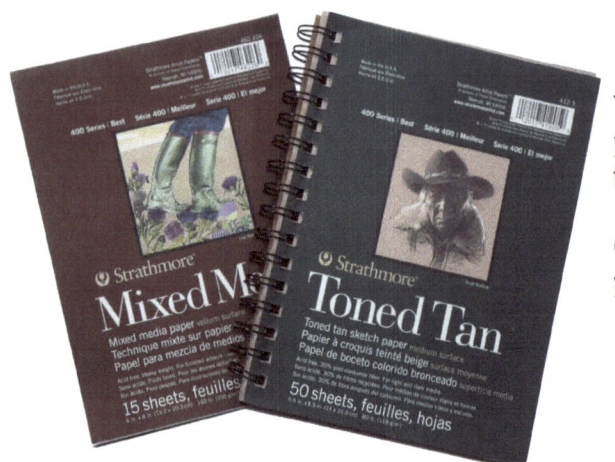

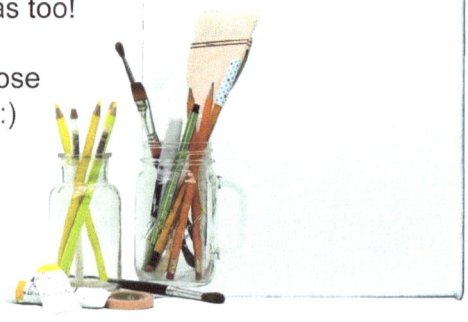

These tips work on any paper you want. If you like to paint, they work on canvas too!

Go ahead and choose your tool of choice :)

One way of transfering is using a lightbox. This works well with paper that isn't too thick.

Don't have a lightbox? No problem! You can use other tools around the house. Perhaps a tablet, a clear clipboard with a lamp, even taping (carefully!) the art to a window and tracing with the sun!

Don't feel like you need all the expensive art tools in order to be creative!

Though if you want to use thicker paper that doesn't show through a lightbox, or cavases, here's a method for you: graphite transfer paper!

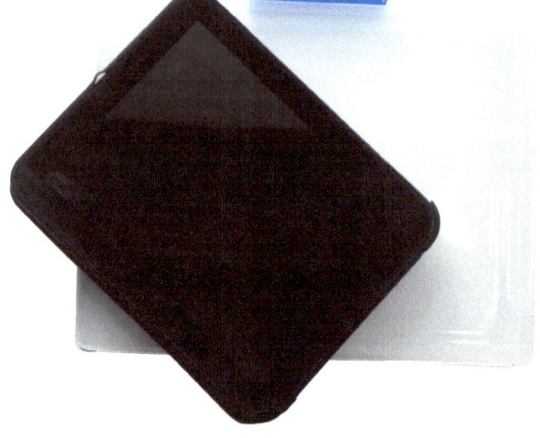

You can buy mass-produced paper or make your own! Just cover the back of a piece of paper with graphite. The more the better!

TIP:

Have newspapers?

Another alternative for the graphite transfer paper is news-paper! If there is a large black ink printed section, you can use that instead!

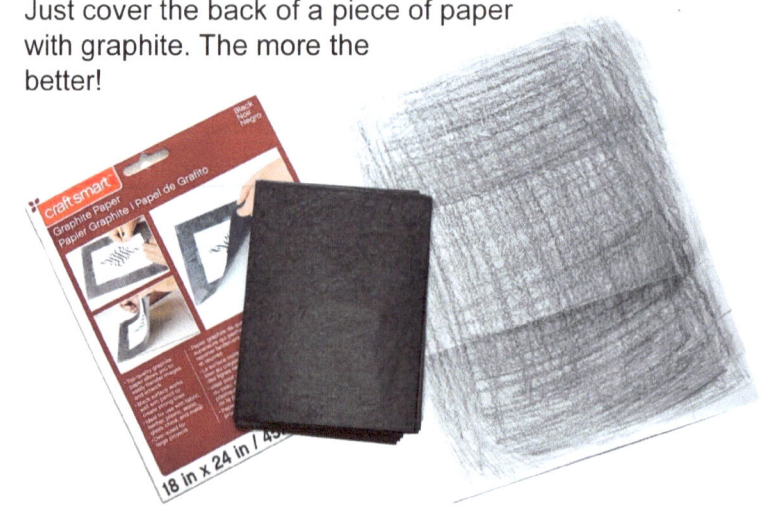

Transfer Tutorial: cont.

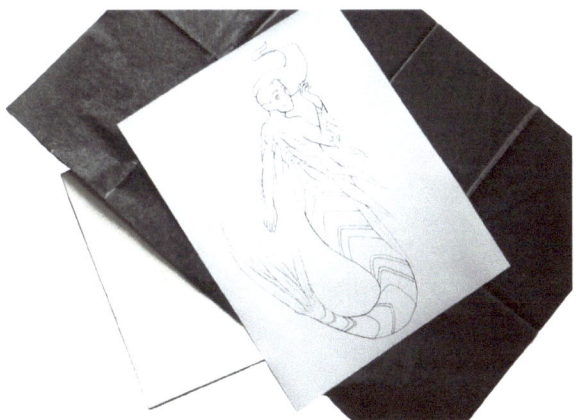

Make a copy of the artwork you wish to transfer. Place it on top of the paper or canvas with the graphite paper in between.

To make sure the papers don't move, you can use tape to hold them in place. (I recommend masking tape as it's softer. To prevent tearing, you can stick it to your clothing a few times to cover some of the glue with lint and clothing fibers.)

The reason you'll want to use a copy of the line art instead of using the original that you purchased (if you have the physical book), is because you'll be drawing over it to trace and transfer. Even if you're not using a marking tool, you'll be slowly indenting the paper over time, and you'll want that in tip-top shape just in case you'll want to color on the original later. (Or in case you want to make future copies to trace and transfer with once that copy starts wearing down.)

You can use most anything to trace over the lines, just make sure it has a point. You could use a pen, pencil, etc., or a blunt toothpick, or other object. You'll want a bit of a fine point for more control and better accuracy.

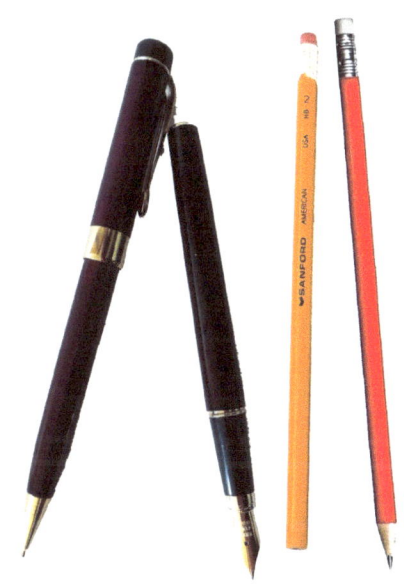

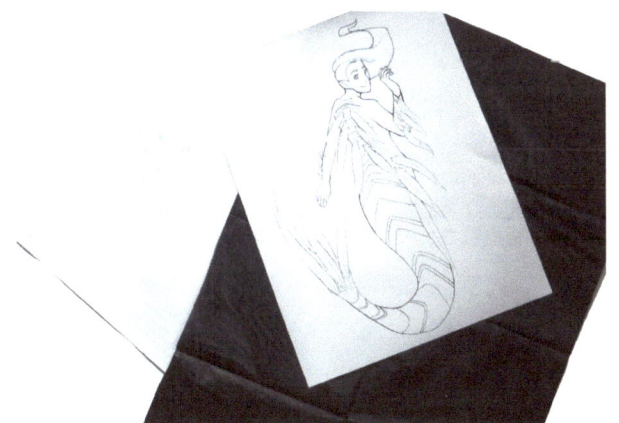

Just take your time. The slower you go and the more you pay attention to detail, the higher the quality of the transferred image will be!

I recommend experimenting with it first before moving on to the real thing, just to get used to the process. You wouldn't want to potentially ruin anything!

If the paper/canvas is larger or smaller than what the artwork is scaled at, you can always enlarge or shrink the line work to fit your needs. You can use programs such as Adobe Photoshop, The GIMP, or use free online tools by Google searching around.

Coloring Basics Tutorial:

Before we get too deep into the coloring tutorials, let's first talk a bit about coloring in general! These tips apply to any medium and for any style! :)

Cel or Hard

Soft or Gradient

Combined!

It's everyone's favorite--spheres! You can shade these line works in a variety of ways, here are just some examples of styles:

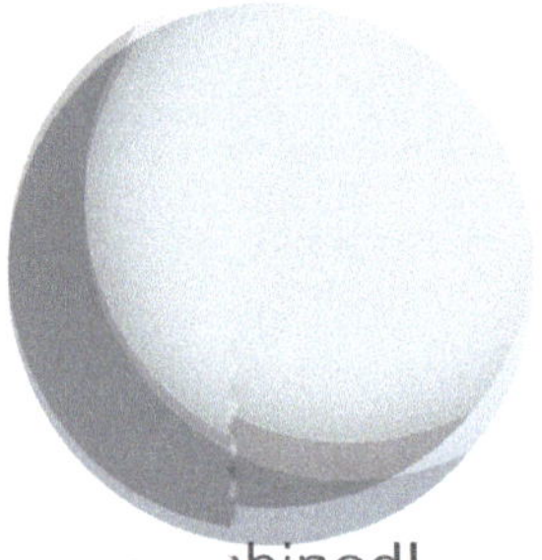

- Highlight
- Midtone
- Core Shadow
- Reflected Light
- Cast Shadow

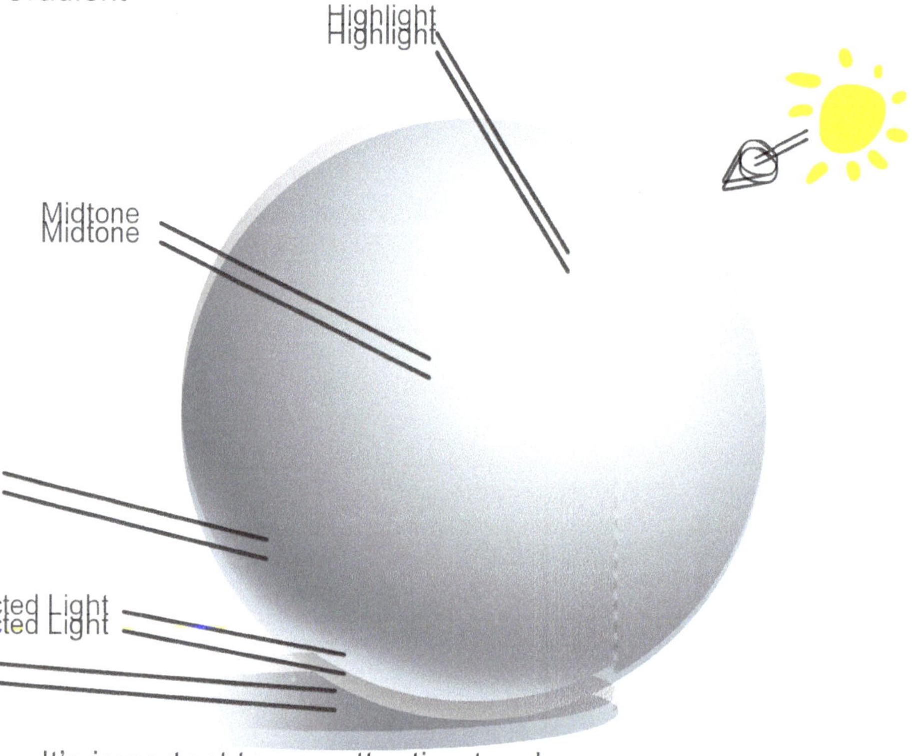

It's important to pay attention to where your light source is coming from, as well as what your light source is. (The sun is drastically different than a camp fire, for example.)

Try to keep the shape and form of the object in mind. Ask how would the light look if cast upon it?

TIP:

Have a ball around?

Grab yourself a ball, or any object really, and use a flash light to shine on it. Turn the lights off and try various angles. Study how the light effects it.

Coloring Basics Tutorial: cont.

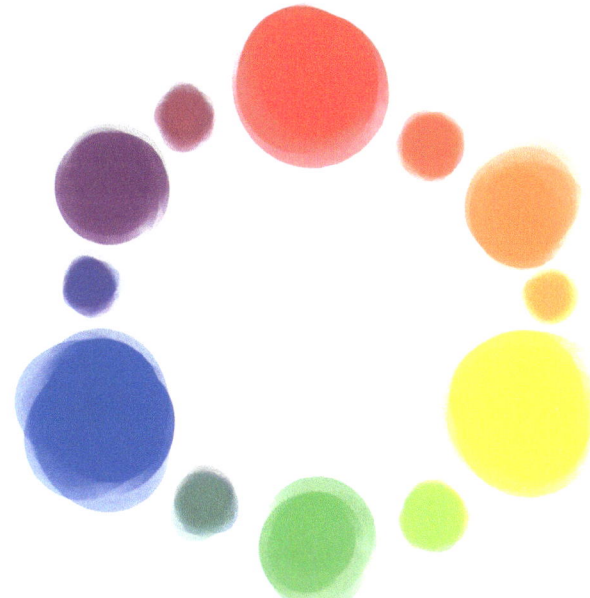

Now let's talk about color! This is the standard color wheel. (The subtractive color wheel.) Red, yellow, and blue are the largest as they are the primary colors.

Secondary colors are made mixing the primary colors together, creating: orange, green, and purple.

Tertiary colors are mixing those colors together, and are represented as the smallest colored circles.

The fancy terms aren't all that important to memorize, but in case you see them referenced in the future elsewhere (especially primary and secondary), you'll know what is being discussed!

Complementary colors are those across from each other on the color wheel. These can be any two colors, just as long as they are directly opposite of each other.

For example: yellow and purple, red and green, blue and orange.

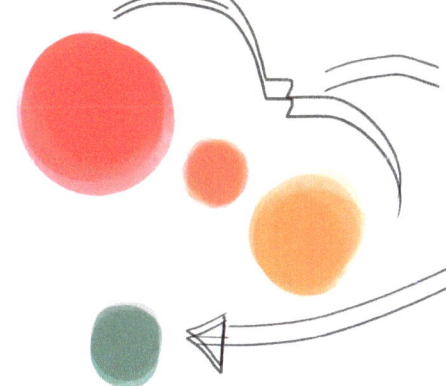

Analogous colors are those next to each other on the color wheel. These are the immediate neighbors.

Pairing them with their complementary can make for a pleasing color palette.

Complementary colors in general work well with each other and I recommend experimenting with them to become more familiar with them.

Having a little knowledge of color theory can make your pieces much stronger and more appealing to the eye!

Coloring Basics Tutorial: cont. 2

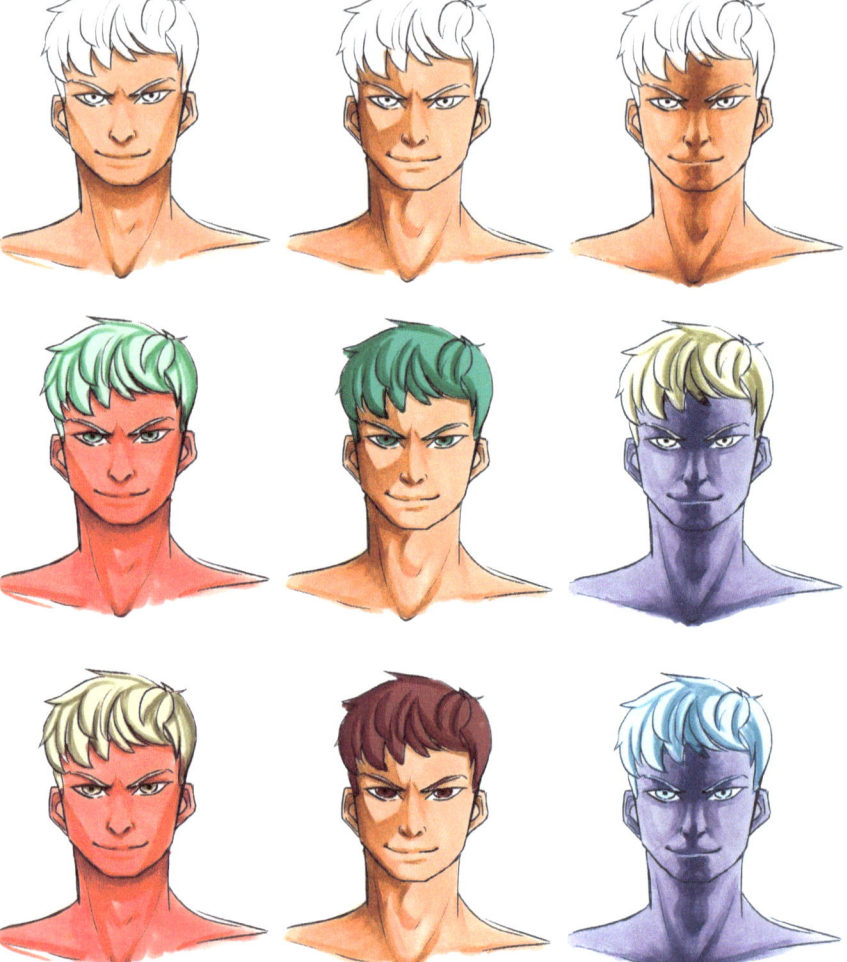

Here are some examples of shading the face using various angles of the light source. Don't over think it. Shading complex objects follows the same patterns and rules and simple ones.

Here are some complementary color combinations.

Red with a light green.
A red orange with a blue green.
And a purple with yellow.

Using analogous colors, we can get a completely different look!

Reds, oranges, and yellows.
And purples with blues.

Try playing around with other color combinations and see what feels right and what doesn't! While there are guidelines in how to create art, there really is no "wrong" way to art. If you want some crazy saturated or wild colors, go for it!

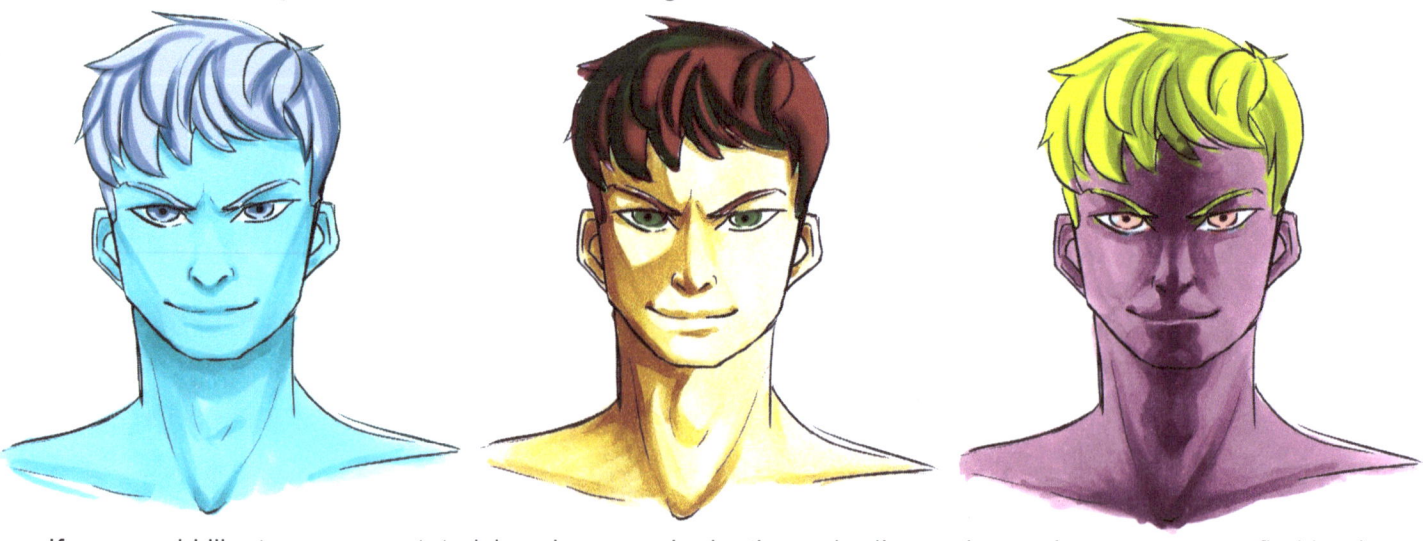

If you would like to see more tutorials going more in depth on shading, color, and more, you can find loads over on my YouTube channel: sambeawesome

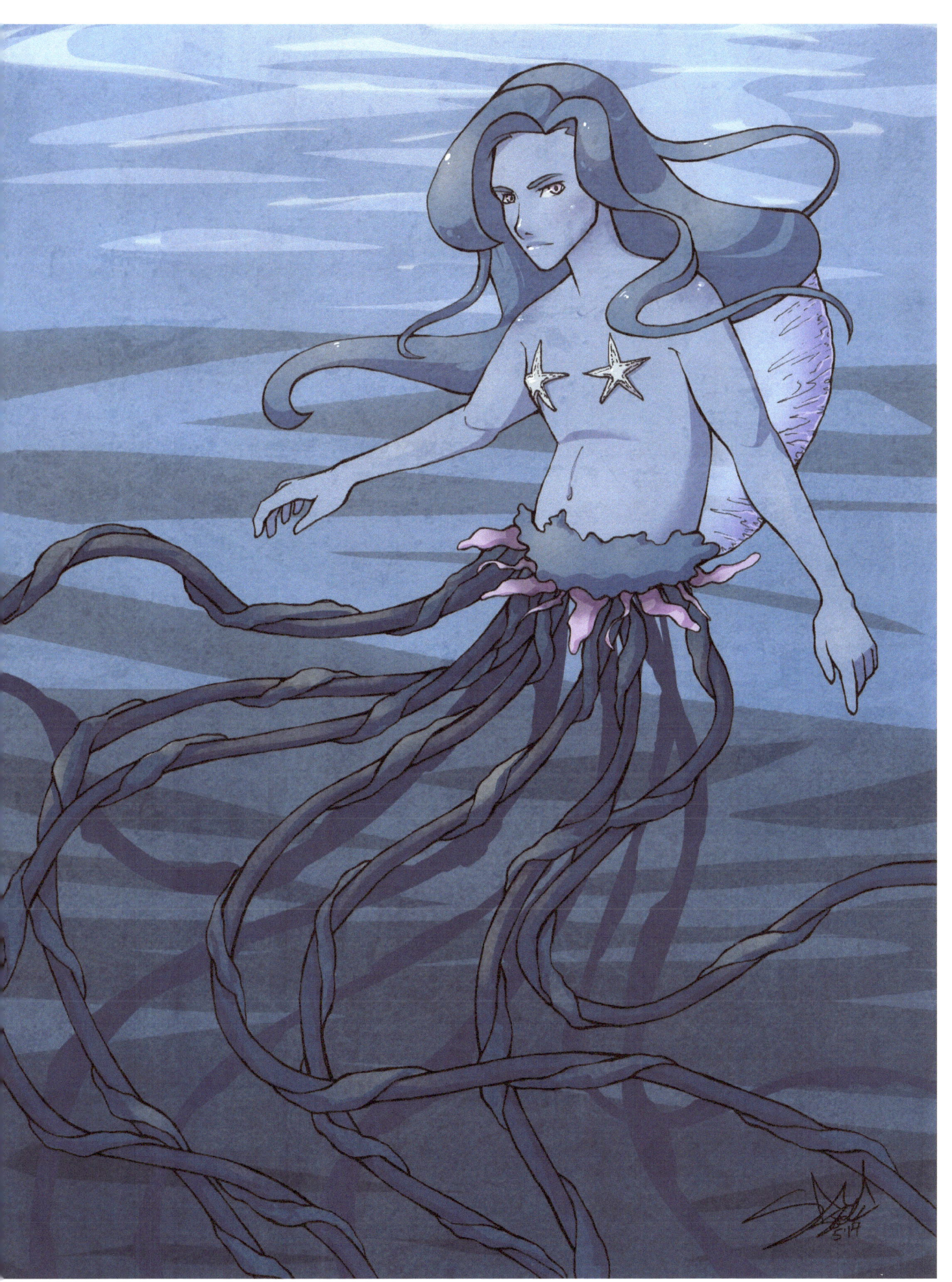

Digital Coloring Tutorial:

It's time to color! I'll be using Adobe Photoshop, but this will be general enough to apply to most any digital arts program.

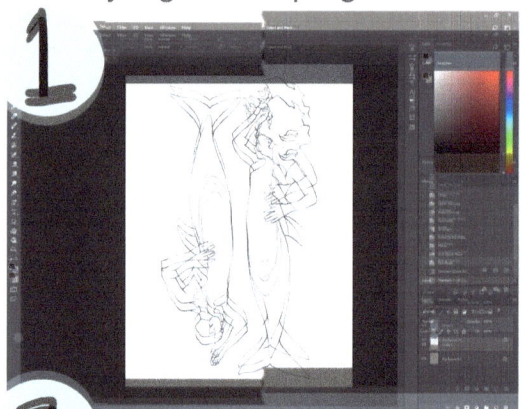

Go ahead and open up the desired file. I've already gone ahead and separated the line work from the white background as described in the transparency tutorial.

My next step is to get a base color down for the mermaids! The initial color doesn't matter, as you can always change it later.

Start off by selecting the magic wand tool.

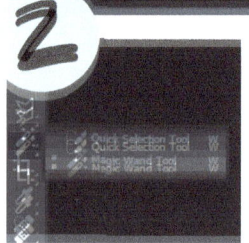
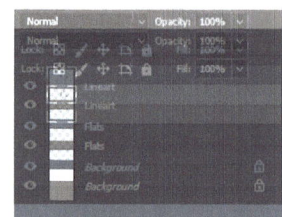

Make a new layer for your flat colors. On your line layer, select all the areas you don't want colored.

(I marked mine in red.)

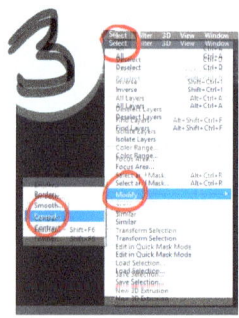
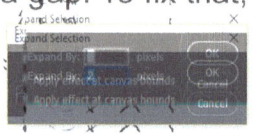

Next, we want to expand the selection. This is because the magic wand tool often doesn't get as close as you might want to the lines, leaving a gap. To fix that, go to Select -> Modify -> Expand.

Two pixels is enough for this size.

You'll then want to invert the selection (CTRL/CMD + Shift + I, or Select -> Inverse) to highlight the area we want filled in. Choose any color and fill in you flats. (Make sure you have the correct layer selected when filling in the color, and don't accidentally fill over the lines!)

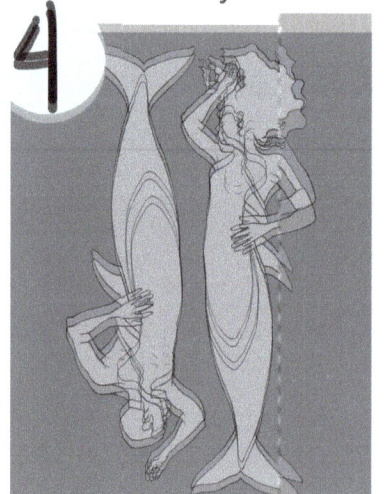

I like to work on a grey background since it helps keep things neutral with my lights and my darks.

Lock your flats layer and adjust the colors to whatever you choose!

I went with the colors of the real striped dolphin :)

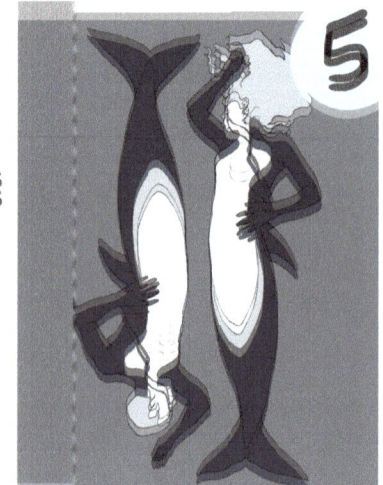

Digital Coloring Tutorial: cont.

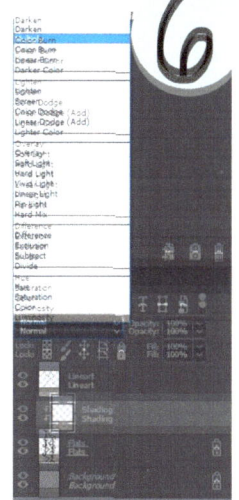

6. Make a new layer above the flats layer for the shading. We'll be using clipping masks. Clipping masks are fantastic for keeping layers grouped together, as well as making sure any work done will stay within the confines that you specify.

Right click the new shading layer and select "Create Clipping Mask" or hold down the ALT key, hover between the two layers, and once the cursor changes to an arrow with a box, left click. Now anything you draw on that layer will stay inside of the area created by the flat color layer!

From there, change the shading layer settings from "Normal" to "Multiply". This will cause anything painted on that layer to darken what's underneath it. This makes for quick and easy shading, which is great for beginners!

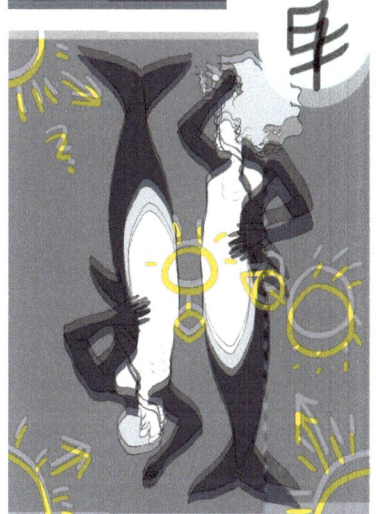

7. Next, decide on a light source! Where is the majority of the light coming from? We need to know as it will tell us how to shade the characters.

I picked the front right. From there, I'm being really messy just laying down color. I'm using the same blue-grey throughout. It doesn't need to look too pretty since I'll be blurrying it.

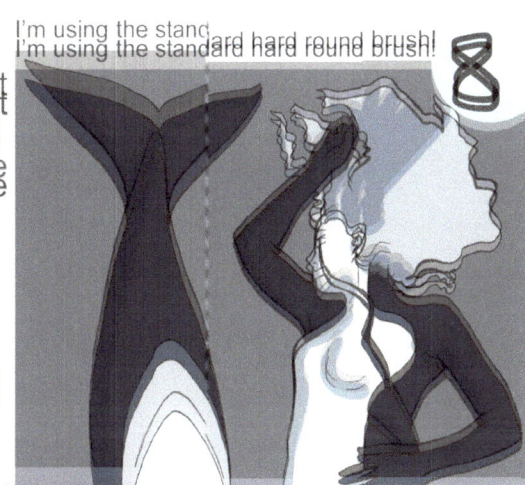

8. I'm using the standard hard round brush!

`#acb7c6`

Now to blur! Go to Filter -> Blur -> Gaussian Blur. I chose 30 pixels, but go with what works best for your artwork.

I don't want this to be too strong, so I lowered the opacity to 50%.

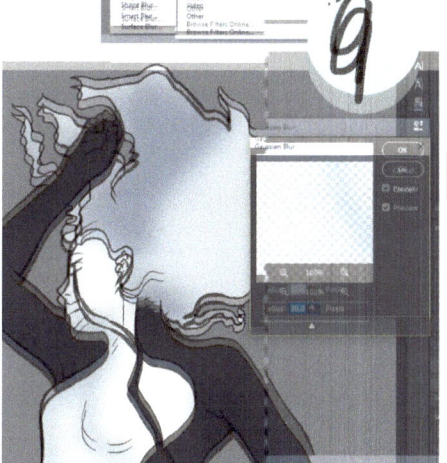

9.

10. Now repeat for the highlights, but use "Screen" instead of "Multiply".

`#b56e27`

I set the opacity to 20%.

I want it to be subtle, not overpowering.

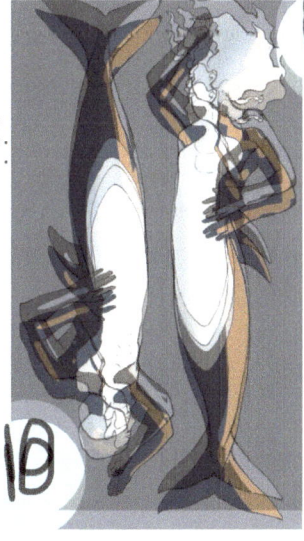

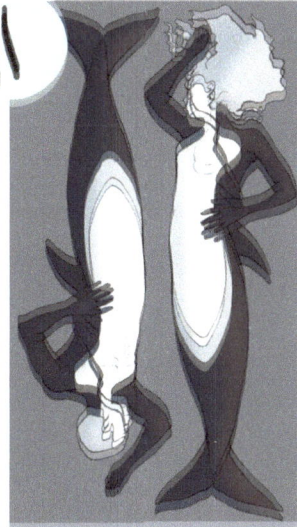

11.

Digital Coloring Tutorial: cont. 2

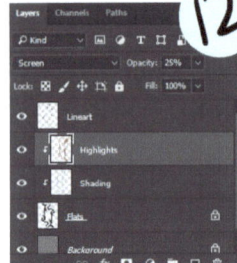

12 We'll be doing some cel shading next. Make a new clipping mask layer and set it to multiply, just like the other shading layer. (See a pattern? Shades go on "Multiply", highlights go on "Screen". You don't have to follow those as rules, I highly recommend playing around with other layer settings and tools your program has to offer!)

Just keep it simple and remember where your light source is coming from.

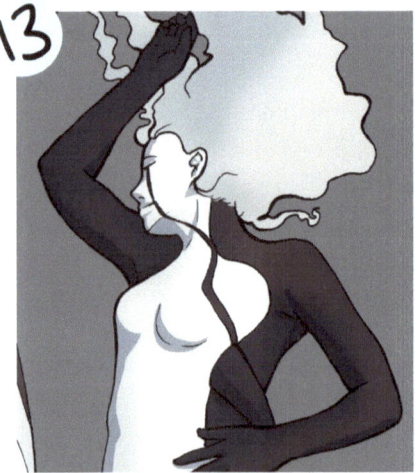
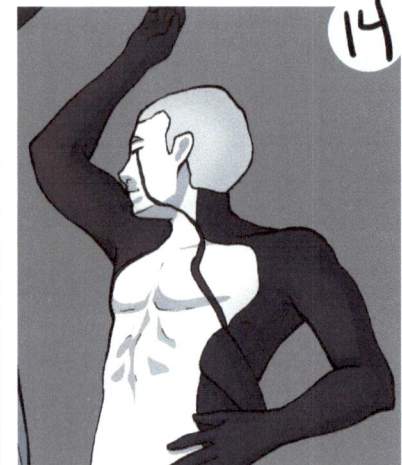

13 **14**

I'm using the same exact blue-grey as before, but because I lowered the opacity of the blurred layer, it still pops out as shading.

Follow the shape and form of the figure/object. Think of the underlying bones and muscles. It's the same as the circles I showed earlier. Break down complex forms into simple shapes to help make shading easier.

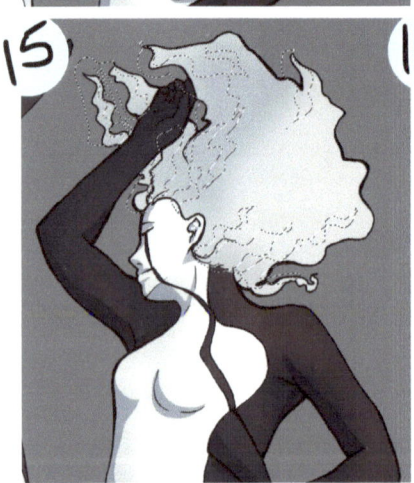
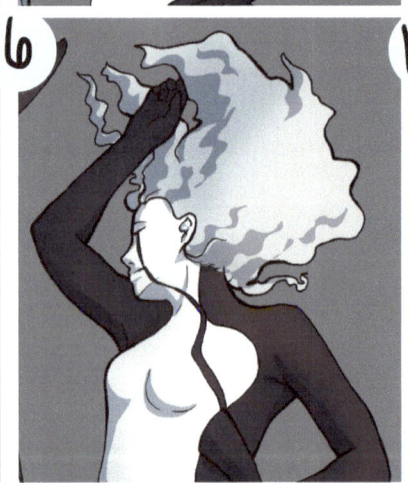
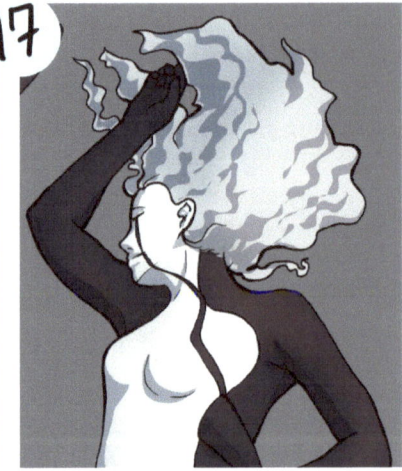

15 **16** **17**

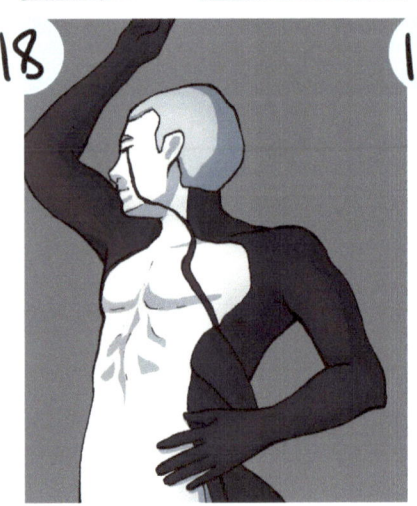
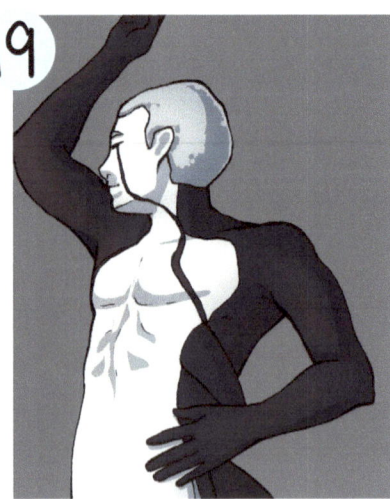

18 **19**

Sometimes I like using the marquee tool, especially if I'm cel shading hair. It gives me some nice and quick fluid lines that have a sharp edge to them. Totally personal preference.

For the guy, I went with a more speckled approach to give it some texture.

Digital Coloring Tutorial: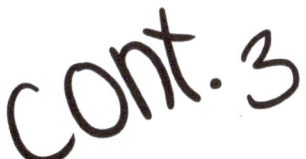

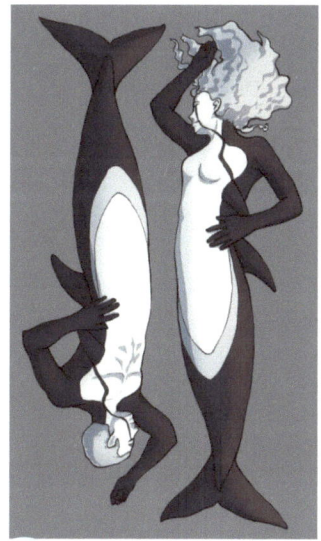
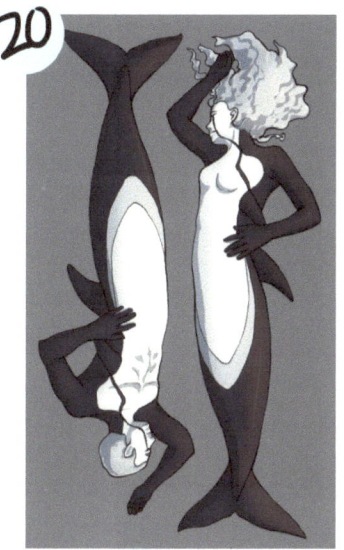

It's time for some highlights! I used the same techniques and tools for the highlights on a new "Screen" layer. I lowered the opacity to 20% so it wasn't too strong.

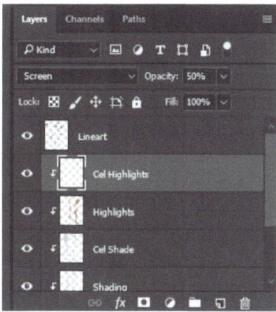

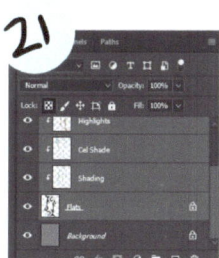
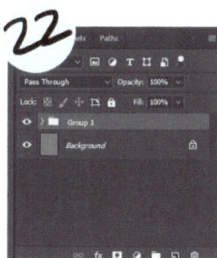
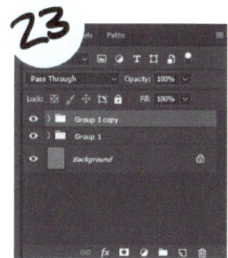
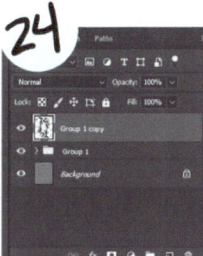
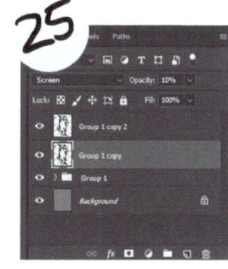
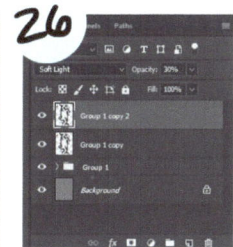

Next is quite a few steps, but don't worry, it's super easy! Select all your current layers (minus any backgrounds) and group them together. (CTRL/CMD + G) Duplicate those layers. (CTRL/CMD + J) Flatten the layers. (CTRL/CMD + E) And duplicate that layer. Flattening them makes the file smaller and your computer happier!

I set the first to "Screen" at 10% since my art is a little dark and I wanted to brighten it up a touch. The second is "Soft Light" at 30%, just to give the artwork a little 'pop'. :) It's really subtle, but it makes a difference!

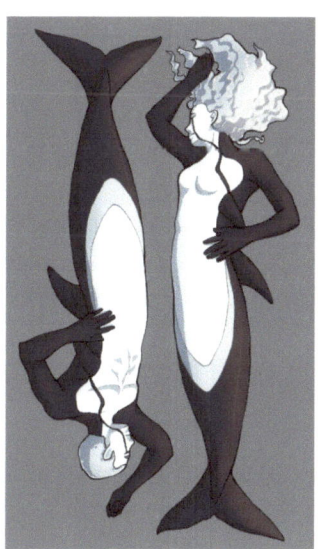

I wanted a bit more of a pop of color, so I made a new layer of "Overlay" and painted on some blue in the shadows and yellow on the highlights.

I blurred using Gaussian Blur, then lowered the opacity to 15%.

It's more subtle alterations, but every little bit adds up. (Plus it can be pretty fun to play around at this stage with the layer settings!)

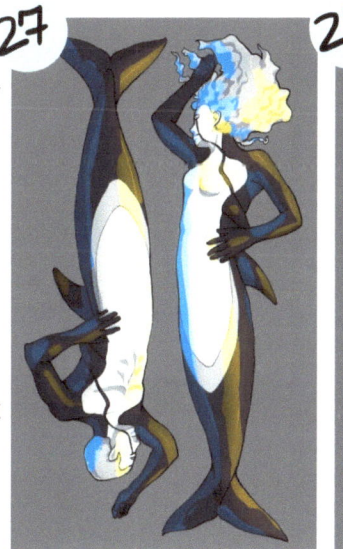
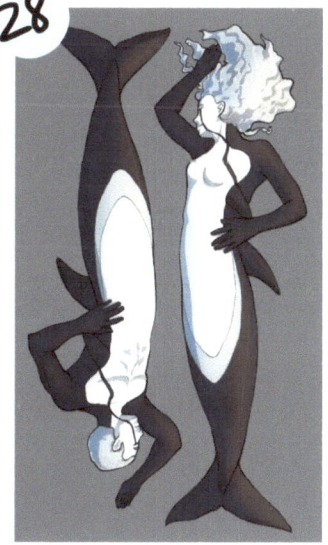

Digital Coloring Tutorial: Cont. 4

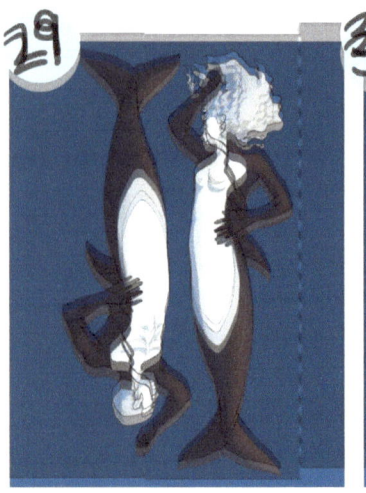 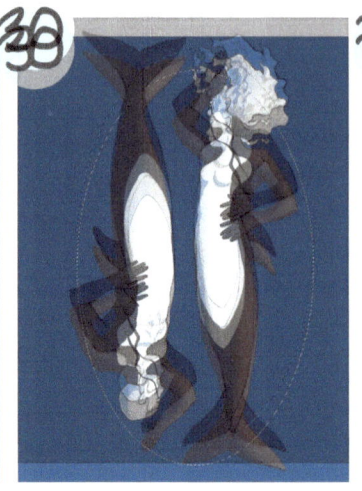 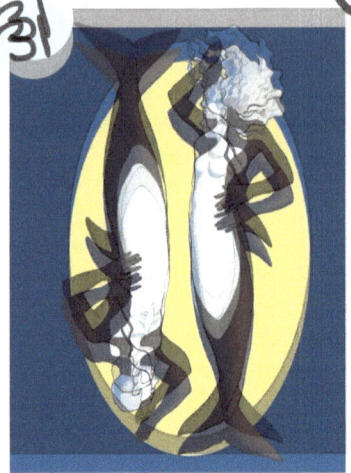 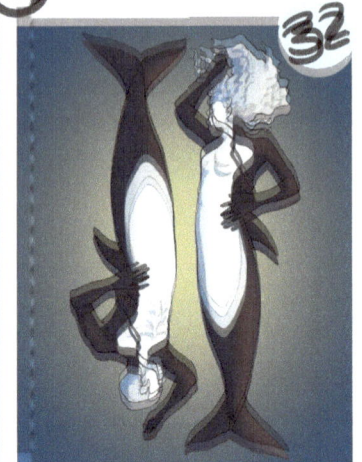

Time for the background! Filled in a dark blue. (#193a67) Next I went in with the circle marquee tool and made an oval in the center. I filled that in with a yellow on a separate layer. (#f4df82)

I'm trying to keep to similar colors throughout the piece to have things feel more balanced and consistent.

Then I blurred the yellow with Gaussian Blur.

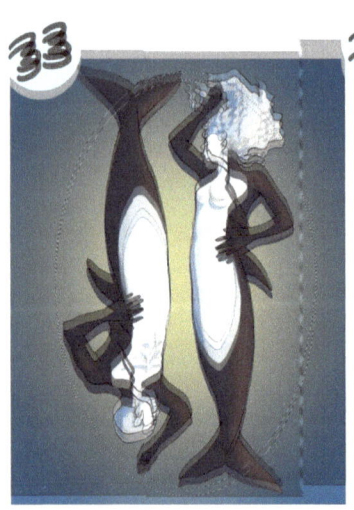 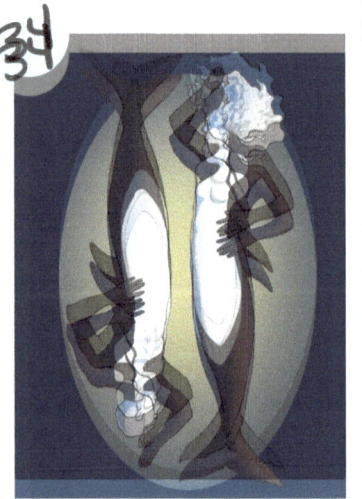 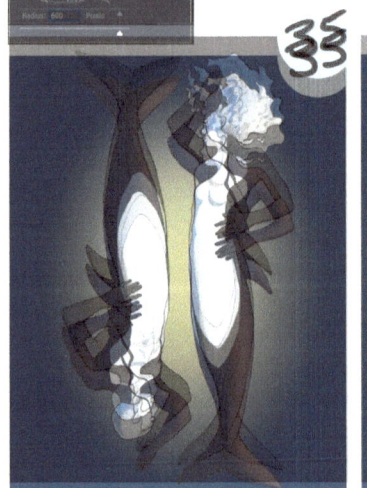 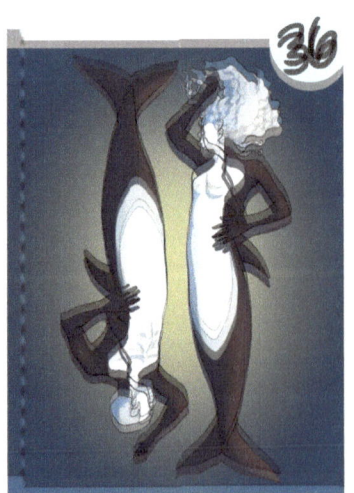

I made another oval on a new layer and inverted the selection (CTRL/CMD + Shift + I) and filled that in with a darker blue. (#0f233f) This helps the center be the brightest point, emphasizing the two mermaids.

I then blurred that layer and lowered the opacity to 50%.
At the end is what my layers box looks like at this point.

Digital Coloring Tutorial: cont. 5

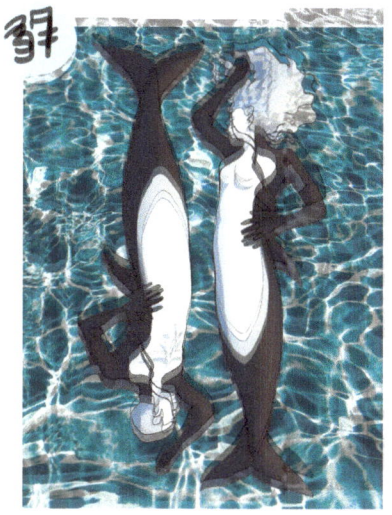 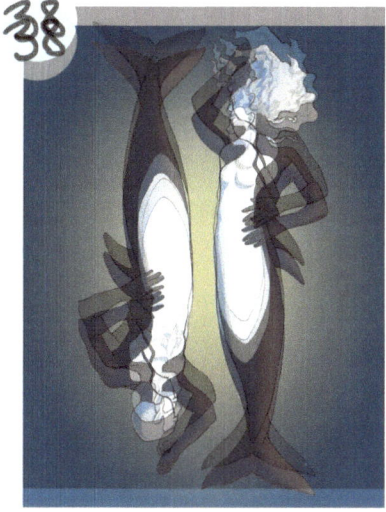

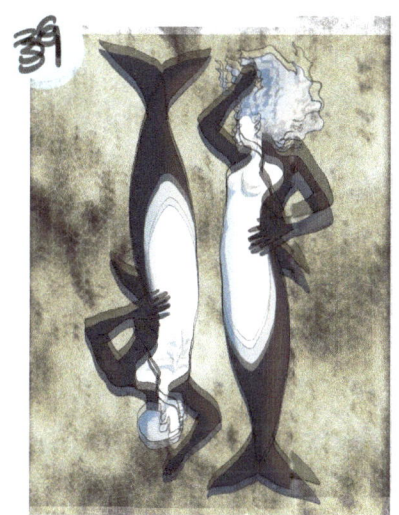 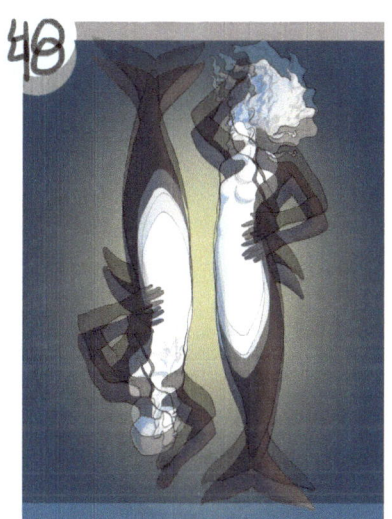

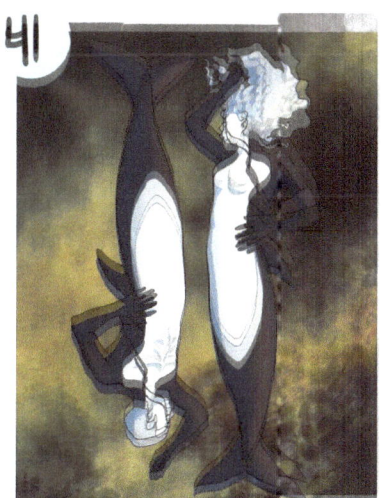 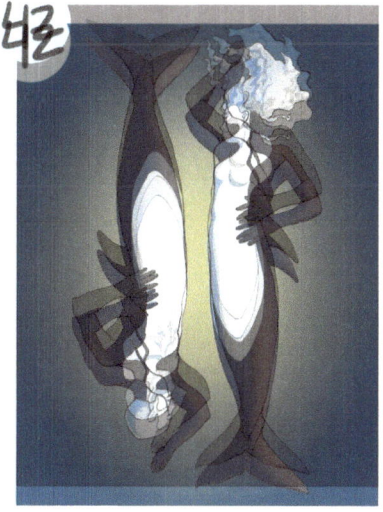

37, 38, 39, 40, 41, 42

Here comes more fun! I added in a couple of random textured images from Pixabay.com (great resource for CC0 stock images) and played around with the layer settings until I got something that appealed to me.

I didn't want the textures to overpower the artwork, just add to it. The focus of this piece should be on the mermaids. The texture just adds a little bit of interest.

For the first, I set the layer to "Soft Light" at 5%.

For the second, I set the layer to "Soft Light" on 5%.

And the third was also set to "Soft Light" (I really like "Soft Light", haha) at 10%.

It's worth it to play around and find out what textures, if any, will work with your piece. Try different textures, layer settings, opacity, and other various effects, and combinations. You never know what you might end up with, it could be pretty cool!

Try not to rely too heavily on textures like these though. They're supposed to add to the piece, not take away from it.

Textures are a great additional subtle way of building up more detail and can make the piece more appealing to the viewer.

For the last step, I just added some sparkles! (Tutorial on my YT channel!)

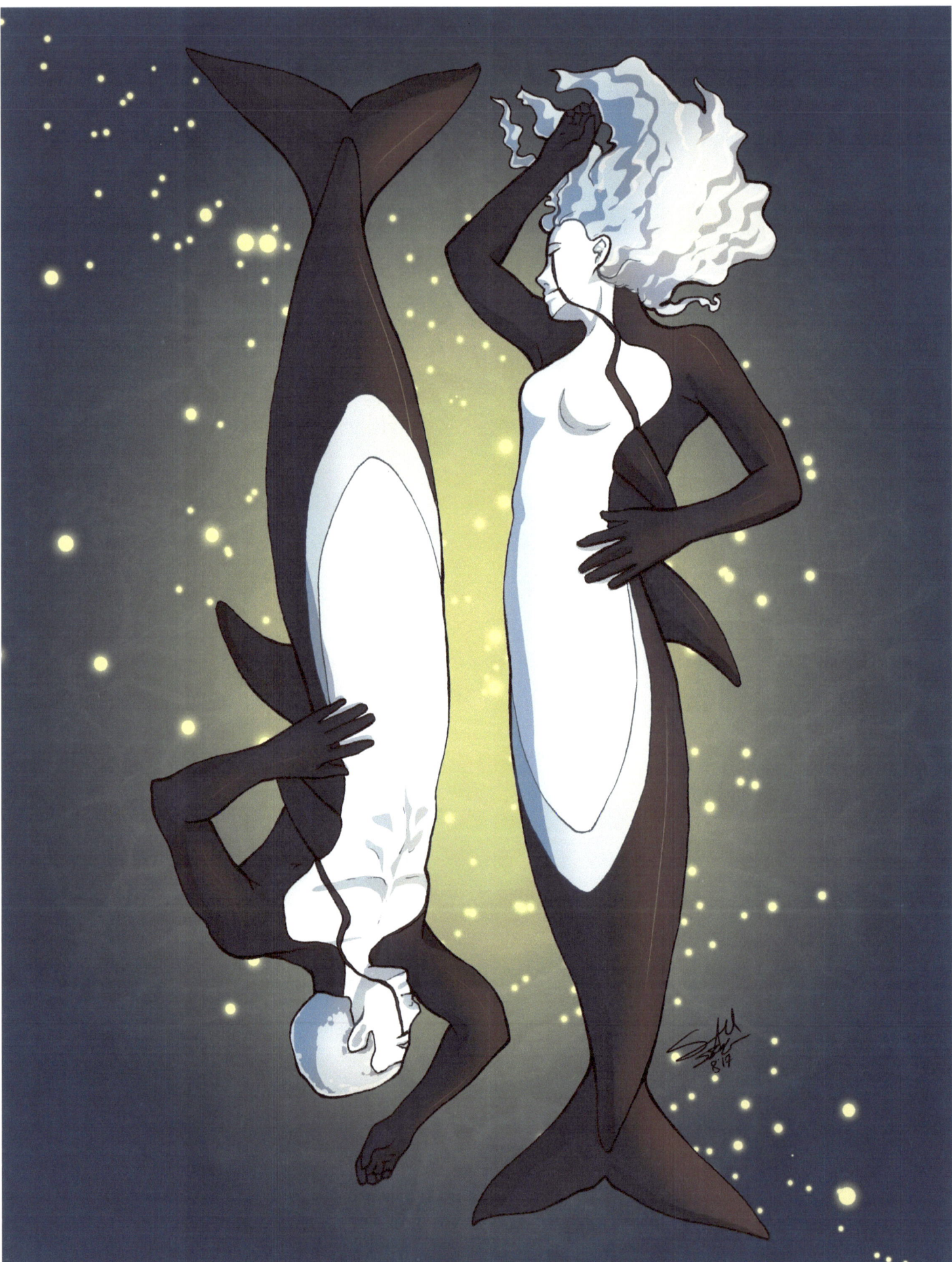

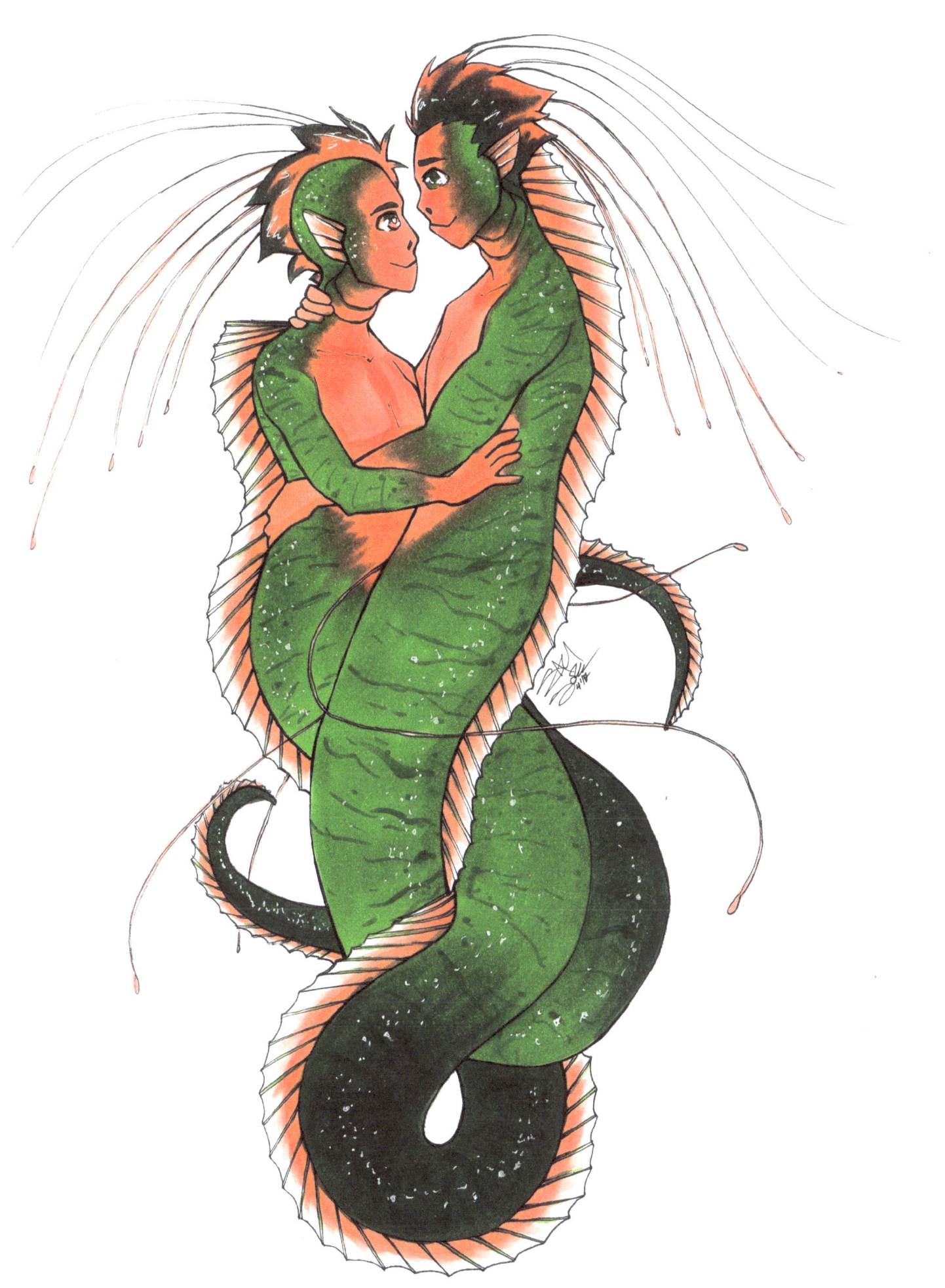

Copic Coloring Tutorial:

It's time to color! I'll be using Copic markers, but techniques will be general enough to apply to most alcoholic markers.

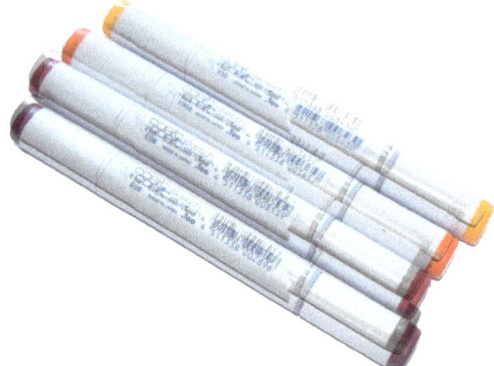

Pretty much all alcoholic markers work the same, though there may be some variation to color options.

A great way to blend with alcoholic markers is by using the 'flick' technique. This is by holding the marker down on the paper with the brush end and moving it in one direction while also lifting off the paper. This has a bit of a 'feather' look to it.

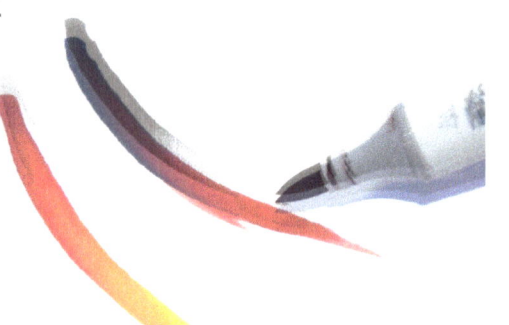

This works well as you can pool a larger amount of ink on one side and have it taper off. When blending more than one color together, you can use this technique to transition the colors.

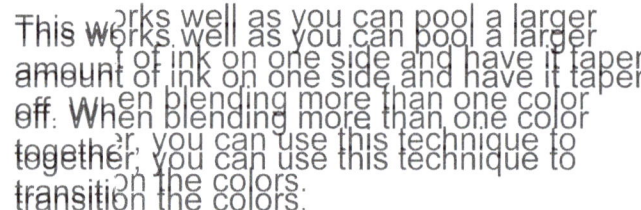

Test out a few flicks and color combinations on a scrap piece of paper and see what you can come up with! As a good test, try blending together complementary colors. Can you go from purple to yellow or red to green smoothly?

In the above picture, I blended: E09, E08, YR04, Y35 in one line, and BV29, W7, E09, E08 in the second line. Don't be afraid to go outside of the color family to mix colors. Often you'll be more lively colors that way.

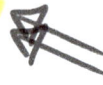

Alcoholic markers depend a lot on layering. If you want to smoothly blend colors, you'll need to go over things a few times.

Take the example to the left with Y35. If your marks look streaky, try coloring in slower and giving the ink time to soak into the paper. Every paper is different, so it'll take some experimenting to figure out what works.

Of course, streaks could make for an interesting texture, depending on what you want! :)

Have rubbing alcohol?

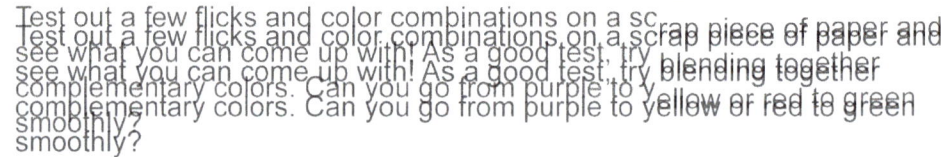

Using high concentrated alcohol like rubbing alcohol with the markers can make for really cool effects!

Try using q-tips or stamps to create textures!

TIP:

Copic Coloring Tutorial: cont.

If you're going to use markers in the physical book, I recommend putting some paper behind the sheet you're coloring or print off a spare copy.

Once you've chosen which piece you want to color, it's time to figure out what colors you want to use!

I picked the lionfish and am using Y35 for the base.

You both want to take your time, to let ink flow smoothly, and go kind of quickly, so it doesn't dry and you get lines where you paused in coloring. It's a 'figure it out as you go' sort of deal, and as I said, it varies with paper and marker type.

I'm using regular computer paper here and I try to work in sections so everything will look as smooth as possible.

Be mindful that markers tend to bleed, ie spread. Test out your paper and markers ahead of time to see how much of a gap, if any, you'll need so it doesn't go outside the lines.

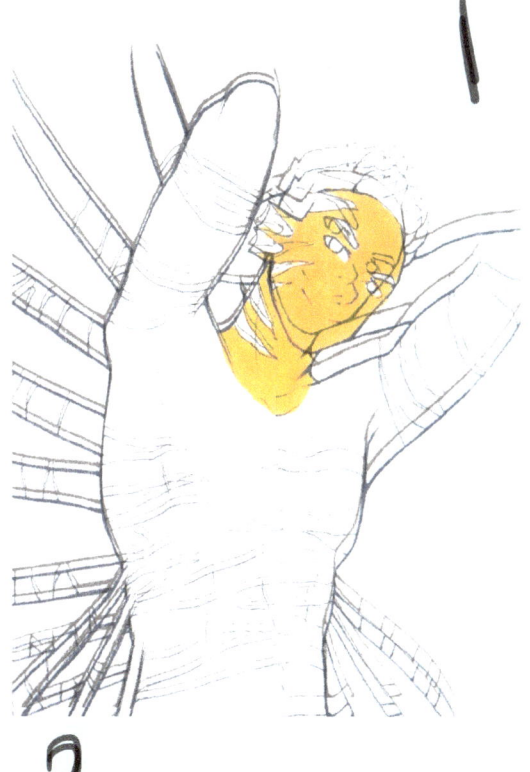

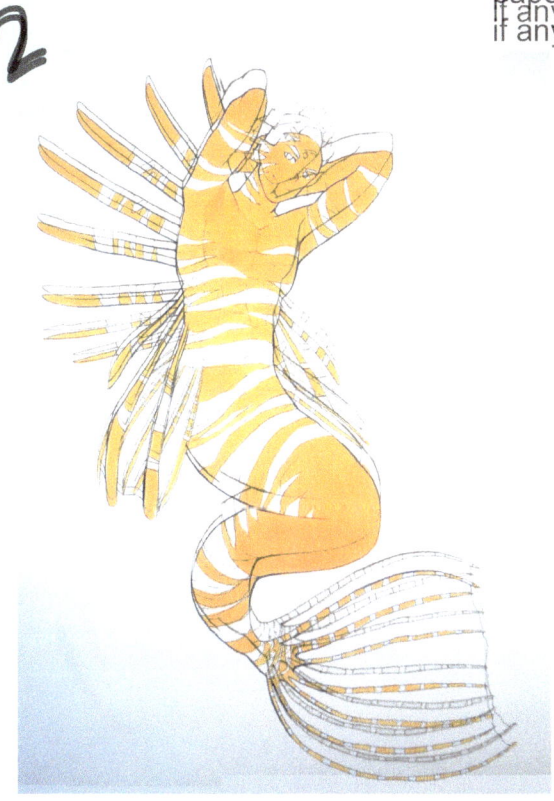

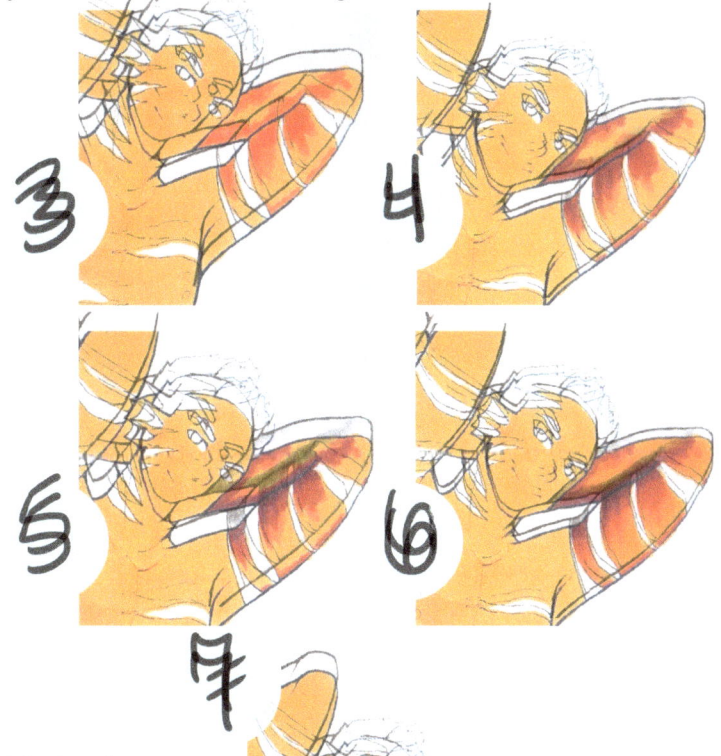

Working on one section at a time so I can blend faster, I use YR04, E08, E09, then go over it all with Y35 again, doing a few touch-up blending with YR04 again to help smoothen the transition. Remember to keep in mind your light source!

Copic Coloring Tutorial: cont. 2

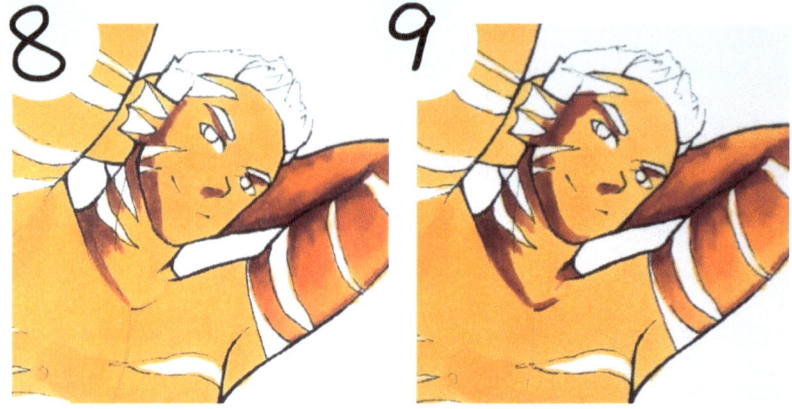

The process continues as I follow a similar pattern throughout. Though I switched from coloring light to dark to dark to light, as I felt the blending process would be easier for me that way.

Experimenting is a great way to find out what works or what doesn't with your drawing process!

I colored E09, E08, YR04, and blended it all out with Y35. Going back and forth between colors can make for smoother blending.

If you want hard edges or cel shading, just mix the colors less and draw in those lines without blending.

After I shaded in his whole body, I went back in with YR04 and added some texture to the skin. I was really shaky and imperfect when adding my lines. I dabbed a large blob then wiggled the brush nib around. (Don't press too hard, you don't want to ruin your nib!)

This adds some more interest and makes things more realistic and appealing. (Well, I think so :P)

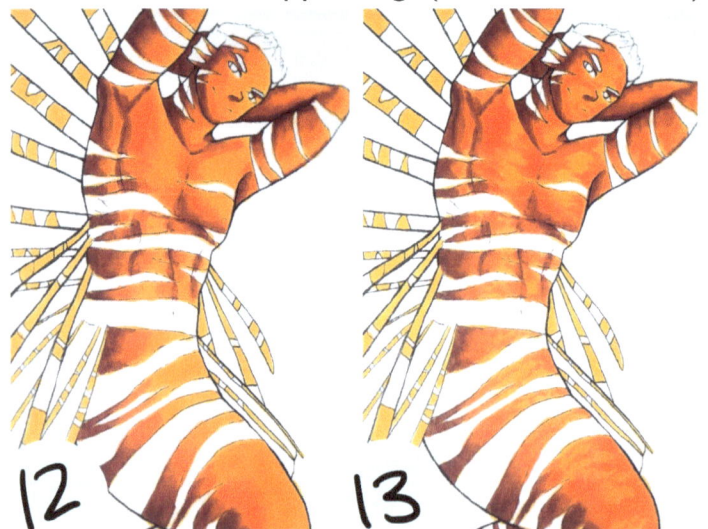

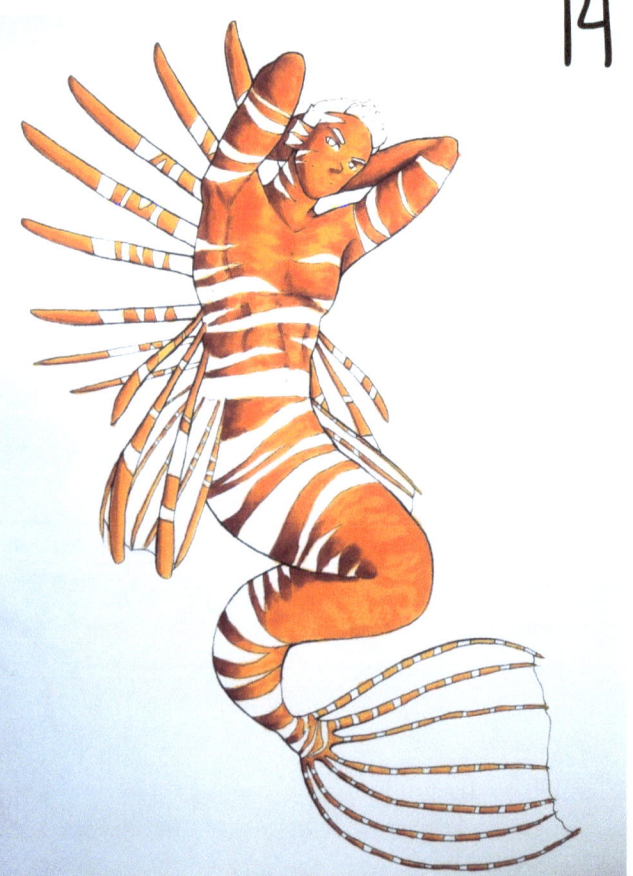

Copic Coloring Tutorial: cont. 3

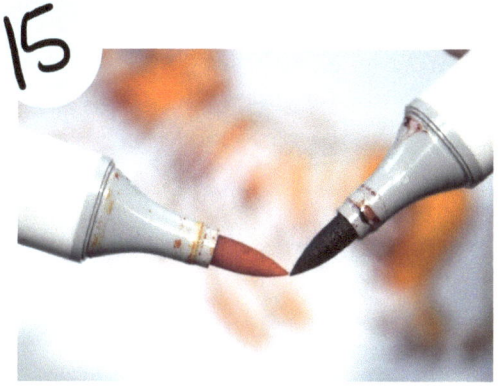

15

A great way to blend two colors together is the "tip to tip" method. This is touching the tips of two markers together, then coloring after. You get a bit of a mix of the two colors and it can be nice to add a bit of subtle darkening, transition, or texture, without having to use the full opaque marker color.

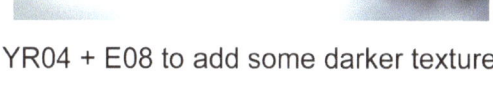

YR04 + E08 to add some darker texture

16

Next, I move on to the paler colors of the fins. I started with E50, then YR20, and went over that with E21. I used flicking and layering to blend them over each other.

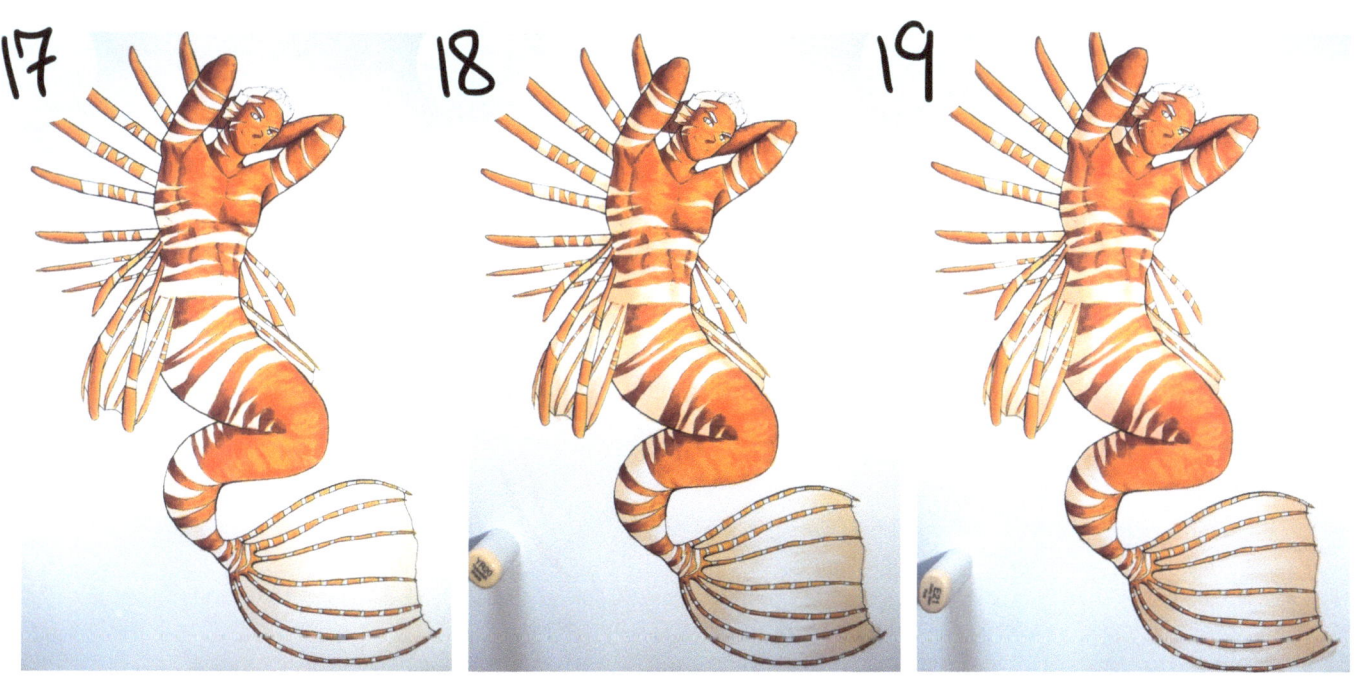

17 18 19

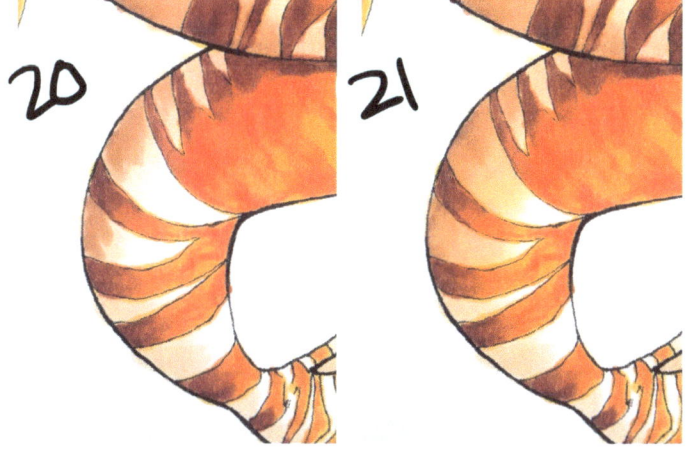

20 21

For my darkest layer, I used E33. Since it was quite a bit darker than my other colors I've used thus far, I went over it immediately after with YR20 to try and smoothen things out for that soft shaded look.

You don't need to use these exact colors, or even anything close to these colors at all. Use what you have or what works best for you!

Copic Coloring Tutorial: cont. 4

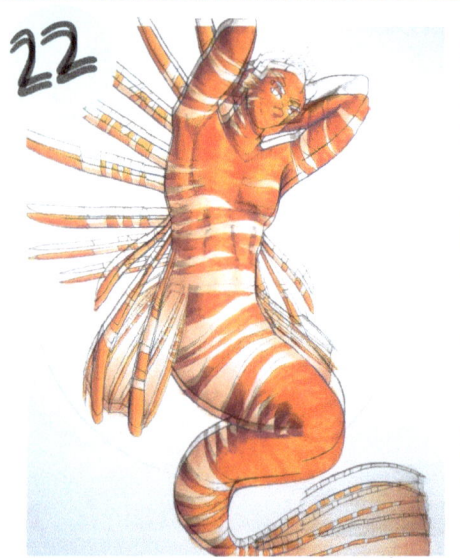

I made a circular background with a bowl I had lying around, but you can also use a CD, a cup--get creative! :) I outlined in pencil so I could erase it later.

I started with black (100) to outline the circle and work my way in a bit. Next I used W7, BV29, and finally B39 to get in some blues to go with the oranges.

For the hair, I used E09, E08, W7, and Y35 for the lightest parts.

To get rid of any stray marks outside the lines, I went over them with my white gel pen. (Sakura Gelly Roll, but any pen is fine!) I also added subtle highlights with the gel pen by dotting it on and dabbing my finger on top to remove some of the ink and soften it.

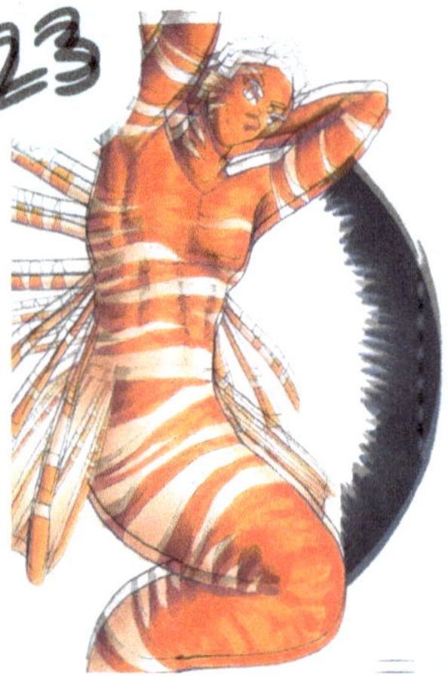

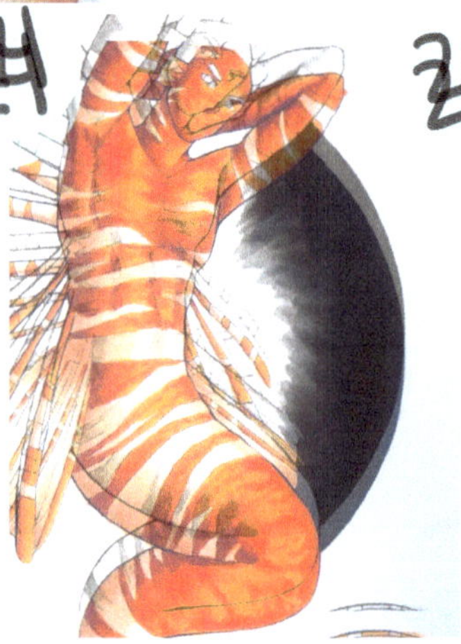

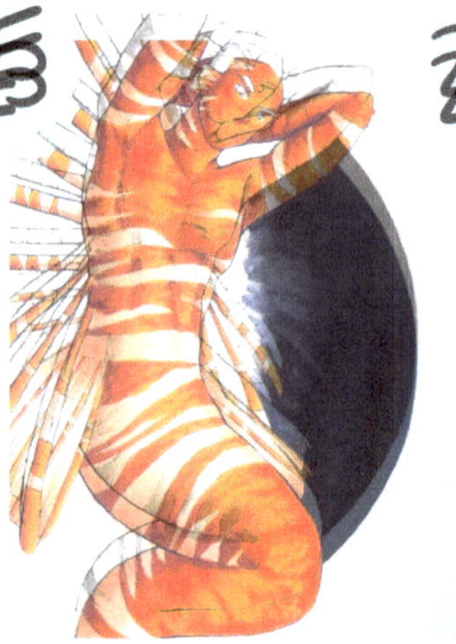

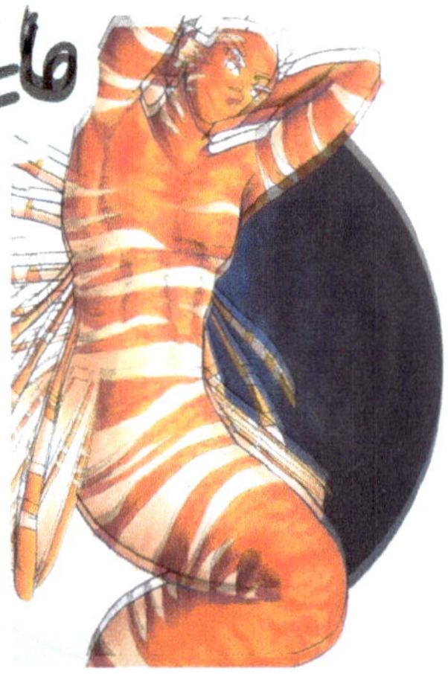

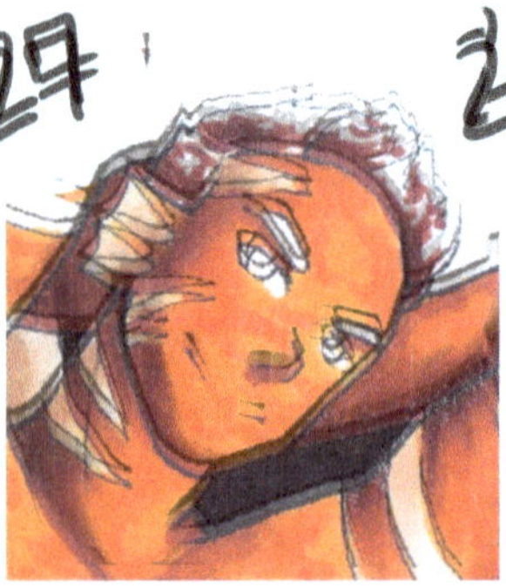

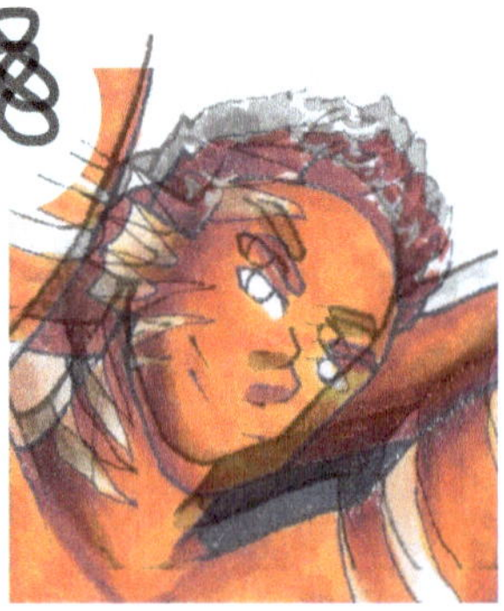

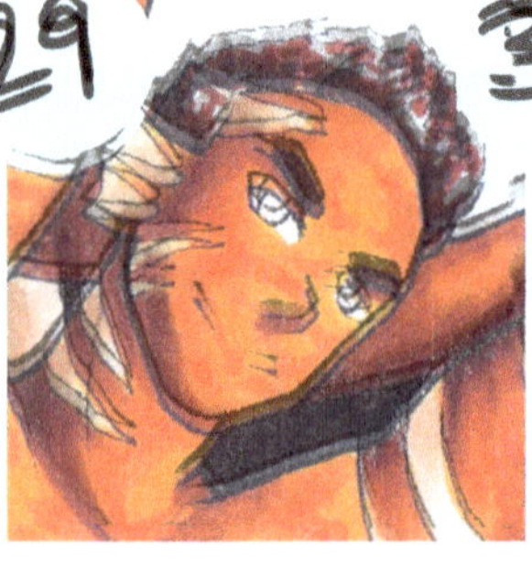

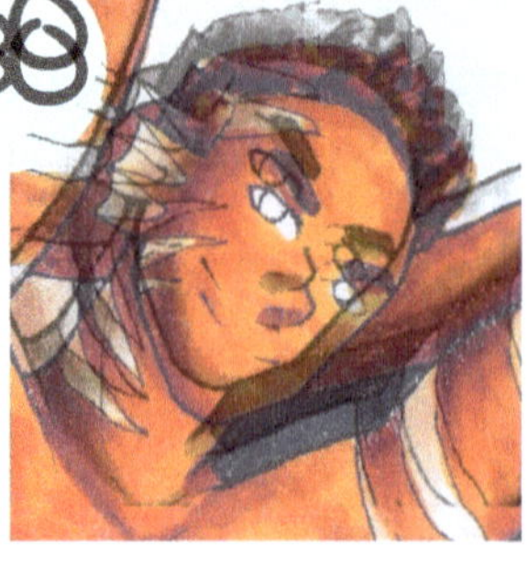

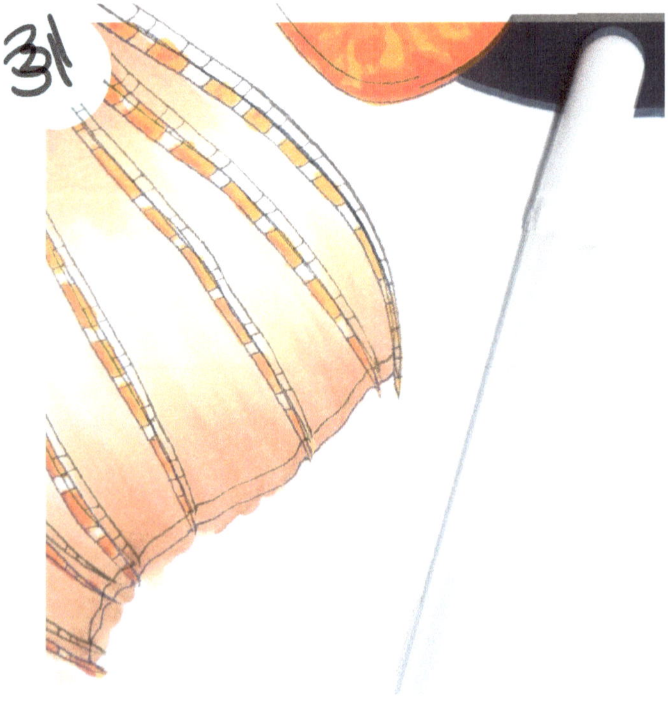

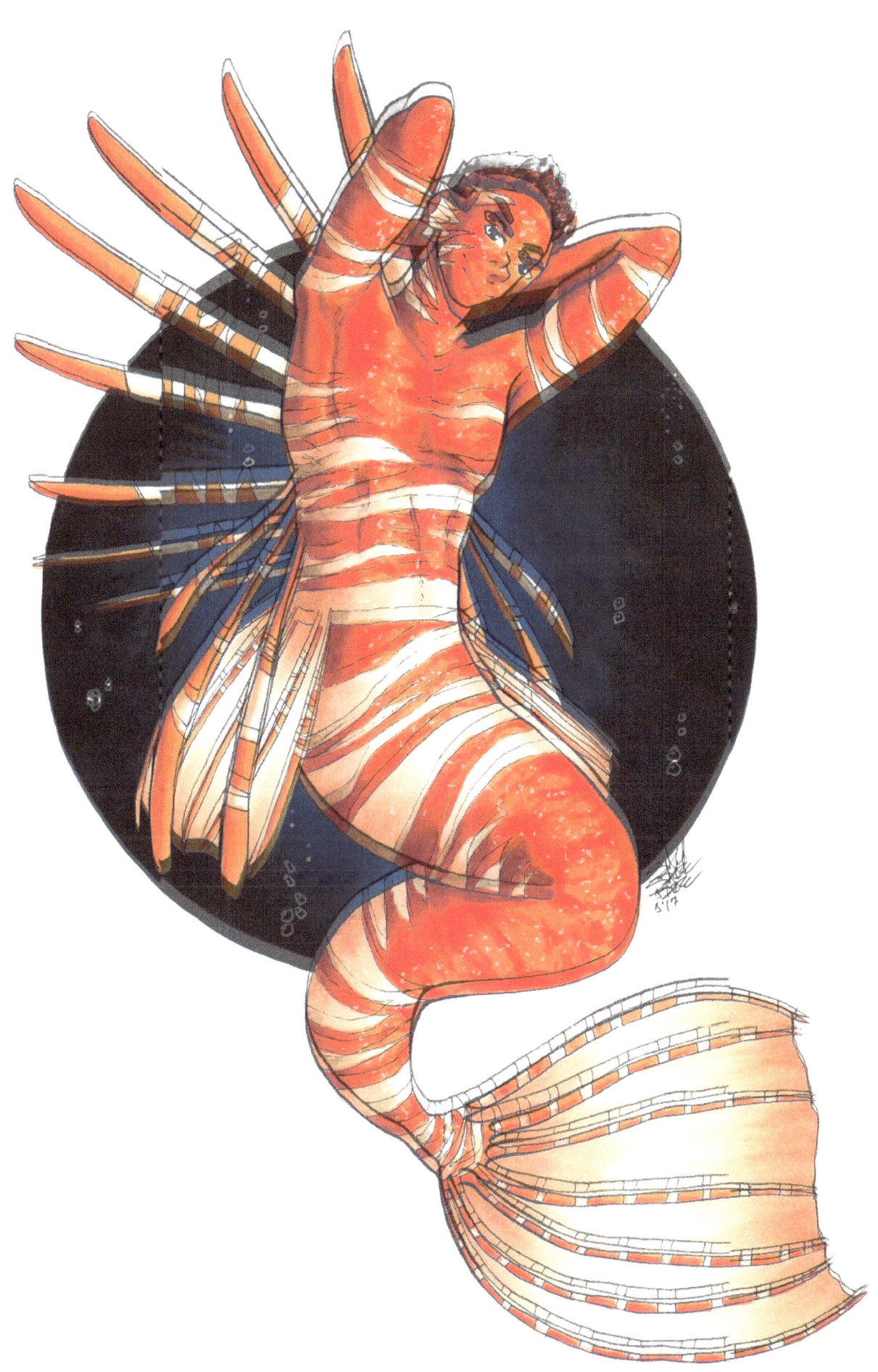

About the Artist

Hello again! Welcome to the back of the book ;) (We hold lots of parties back here, shh, don't tell the front pages, can't have them getting jealous.)

In case ya' didn't know, my name is Samantha Segal. I was born and raised in Florida, US. (Yes, *that* Florida. We know.) I've been interested in the arts as far back as I can remember. My mom was the one who helped me pursue the craft and I've been non-stop on the improvement train ever since. I work hard every day to get better and better, trying to reach new heights. It's kind of an obsession, haha.

If you're interested in finding more of my work, you're guaranteed to find me by looking up my username: sambeawesome.

But if you're lazy (I know the feeling), you can find me on these specific pages below:

Deviantart: sambeawesome
YouTube: sambeawesome
Twitter: sambeawesome
Facebook: sambeawesome
Instagram: sambeart
Tumblr: sambeart

Thanks so much for purchasing my book and helping to support my passion! I greatly appreciate having this opportunity, and people like you make it possible for me. So really, thank you! <3

www.ingramcontent.com/pod-product-compliance
Lightning Source LLC
Chambersburg PA
CBHW051917210526
45473CB00006B/2048